"Intensely practical and deeply insightf [of book] I would've loved when I was a young parent desperate for wisdom from parents who have been there. The Schuknechts have an uncanny ability to help you discern what to do in many child-rearing situations—all with grace and peace. Any parent wanting to instill a godly heritage in their children's lives should read this book."

—MARY DEMUTH, author of *Building the Christian Family You Never Had*

"With the gentleness of grandparents and the wisdom of professionals, Glen and Ellen tell heartwarming and inspiring stories that give practical insight into grace-filled child-rearing. Applying their insights will prepare kids for life in the real world and pass a rich heritage of faith to the next generation."

—JIM JACKSON, president and cofounder of Connected Families

"This book is more than a nice theory that academics came up with while writing in their book-lined offices. I've seen the godly heritage that Glen and Ellen have built in their family. I've pulled up a stool to their kitchen counter, eaten Ellen's famous cinnamon rolls, and eavesdropped on the holy conversations that they've had with their kids and grandkids.

"So much of the teaching I received as a parent was about breaking a child of their sin. But along with trying to break the sin, we sometimes broke their spirit. That is why I cannot recommend this book enough. Discipline while building up a child's faith instead of breaking their spirit? Yes, please!

"A must-read for every struggling parent and grandparent who wants to leave a spiritual legacy and feels that it might be too late. The good news? It's never too late to show God's love to our kids."

—KATHI LIPP, best-selling author of *Overwhelmed* and *The Husband Project*

"I am incredibly blessed to have grown up with parents who gave me a true spiritual heritage—one that carried me through my tough teenage years and into adulthood, where I have started my own family. I can't recommend this book enough to parents and grandparents who want to build strong, connected families that will love God and love each other."

—ERIN MACPHERSON, author of more than 12 books including The Christian Mama's Guide series and *Put the Disciple into Discipline*

"If God has blessed you with children, they are your most important calling. They are immortal souls entrusted to your care. Will your children love God? Will your grandchildren make a difference in the world for Christ? Glen and Ellen's book is filled with powerful Scriptures, honest stories, and everyday ideas that will equip you to shape the faith of your family for generations to come."

—DR. ROB RIENOW, founder of Visionary Family Ministries

"Glen and Ellen Schuknecht give parents and grandparents a wealth of ideas and practical tips that will help them achieve the crucial personal connections that are the bedrock of strong families and strong faith.

"Instead of a list of rules, the Schuknechts offer fresh approaches and principles that readers will be excited to apply. Their stories filled with humor, warmth, and authenticity make this an entertaining read, as homey, comforting, and encouraging as the first bite of a warm cinnamon roll. Recipe for success definitely included!"

—MARTHA SINGLETON, coauthor of *The View Through Your Window*

"Glen and Ellen Schuknecht have written a beautiful, hands-on book about building the kind of family we all dream of having. There is no formula here (because that doesn't exist, of course), but there are many helpful ideas for connecting the hearts of each person in your family to one another and to the grand heart of God. These chapters are full of hope and vision. For those of us who did not come from families with deep spiritual heritages, their advice gives shape to the love we long to see play out in the future generations of our own family. We will be forever grateful for their guidance and wisdom."

—MORGAN AND CARRIE STEPHENS, Mosaic Church, Austin

A
Spiritual
Heritage

A
Spiritual
Heritage

Connecting Kids and Grandkids to God and Family

GLEN AND ELLEN SCHUKNECHT

Kregel
Publications

We dedicate this book to our three children,
Erin, Troy, and Alisa, and to their spouses,
Cameron, Stephanie, and Peter,
who are responsible for passing on a spiritual
heritage to our eleven grandchildren,
Josiah, Kate, Jude, Hadassah, Greta, William,
Isaac, Asa, Elsie, Alma, and Bethlehem.

Contents

Acknowledgments

WRITING THIS BOOK AS a husband-wife team has been an inspirational project, one that has certainly motivated us to become even more intentional about passing along a spiritual heritage to our children and grandchildren.

We have a number of individuals to thank, but first we want to acknowledge our eldest daughter, Erin MacPherson, who willingly guided us through the process of writing. She edited each chapter, infusing life and laughter into our stories and ideas. Without her, this book would have remained unwritten.

We would like to express our gratitude to the following people for their support and encouragement, as well as their insights and ideas:

To Troy and Stevi Schuknecht and Peter and Alisa Dusan, who listened to our ideas and supported us with sound advice and encouragement.

To our grandkids whom we love so very much and who provided us with ample stories and illustrations: Josiah, Kate, Jude, Hadassah, Greta, William, Isaac, Asa, Elsie, Alma, and Bethlehem.

To Sarah Joy, our agent who advocated for us, making this journey possible.

To our editors, Janyre Tromp and Dawn Anderson, who painstakingly read our manuscript and offered up wise counsel.

To the employees at Kregel Publications, who believed in us enough to give this book a chance.

To our beloved families and friends at Veritas Academy, who have shared their lives with us on a weekly basis.

We are deeply grateful for each one of you. You have inspired us and made this book possible.

Introduction: Cinnamon Rolls at Oma's

Ellen

I WAKE UP BEFORE the sun rises to make cinnamon rolls. It's a low-key Saturday, so I have invited family over for breakfast. They all live nearby, and it's a privilege to host them when it works with everyone's schedule.

I carefully measure yeast and sprinkle it into tepid water with a teaspoon of sugar. I pull the flour out of the pantry, eyeing the canister to see if there is enough for a triple batch. Last time, my ten-year-old grandson asked for more as he scraped leftover gooey cinnamon off the bottom of the pan, so I quickly add more yeast and water, mentally calculating a triple portion of each ingredient.

As I roll out the dough onto my countertop, I pray for each of my three adult kids and their spouses, and then I pray for my grandkids. There are eleven of them—if you can believe it—ranging in age from one to ten. As I pray, the sun begins to rise over the hilltop outside our house, reds and oranges providing a backdrop for the bare-branched trees, which will soon be covered in blooms and leaves.

The clock reads 6:05 when I slide three white cloths over three large pans of cinnamon rolls so they can proof. By the time the dough begins to rise, my house will likely be full of giggling children and messy-haired adults asking for coffee. And so, I take a minute to relish the silence, the quiet of a still-sleepy morning.

I am not wrong. At 6:25, the first knock sounds at the door. It is my five-year-old grandson, Will, wearing football pajamas and blue flip-flops, his blond hair sticking out at all angles.

"Hi, Oma!" He steps inside before I can invite him in, and hugs my legs. "Can I go wake up Opa?"

Will and his Opa have a special bond, and ever since Will earned the privilege of walking down to our house alone on Saturday mornings, my poor husband hasn't been able to sleep past seven o'clock.

But Glen doesn't mind. It's fun watching him be a grandfather. He was a great dad—the kind who played baseball in the yard and taught the kids to plant a perfect garden. But as a grandfather, he's incredible. My wide-eyed grandsons watch in awe as he goes about his day. They consider each of his daily tasks a heroic feat achievable only by the superhero that is their grandpa. When he mows the lawn, the simple sound of the mower draws a gaggle of preschoolers, each waiting patiently for the chance to ride a loop on his lap. And when he grills on the patio? Let's just say that my ten-year-old grandson, Joey, has figured out how to finagle a second dinner.

As Will trots off to Opa's room with plans to sneak up on him and scare him awake, I glance up the hill to see if any other tiny feet are walking toward my house in the morning sunshine. Sure enough, Will's siblings—Joey, mentioned above, and eight-year-old Kate—are heading down with their coats hastily thrown over their pajamas. On arrival they ask if I want to play a game of Parcheesi. I do, but I tell them I have to get breakfast ready first.

While I wait for the oven to preheat, I grind coffee beans. My son and his wife brought me a ten-pound bag of coffee from Ethiopia, where they finalized their adoption. The beans are rich and fragrant, and just smelling them makes me think of my precious grandson Isaac, and my heart jumps a little. He's just adorable—and while I know I am biased, he is, in my opinion, one of the smartest, spunkiest kids I've ever met. It's still hard to believe that he is ours.

The coffee is brewing, and the timer dings to signal that the oven is preheated. I slide the rolls in just as my son-in-law Peter, who lives next door, walks through the door with his three wily youngsters, Asa, Alma, and Beth. The kids scream and start to run around the couch, chasing each other while throwing a tiny basketball back and forth. Peter steps in front of them and catches them in his wide arms. He sends them off to the back playroom to build Legos with Will.

I return to the kitchen and start scrambling eggs. Haddie, Peter's eldest, joins Joey and Kate at the small game table, and they begin an animated game of Parcheesi. Twenty minutes later, the timer dings, and little feet run into the kitchen. The smells of cinnamon and bacon draw everyone to the table. We crowd around, jostling each other as we fill paper plates with rolls and bacon, and as adults refill their coffee cups. The kids tear into cinnamon rolls with their hands, creating a sticky mess of my clean tabletop. It's loud, frantic, chaotic—and joyful.

This crazy-busy, family-filled life of mine may seem a bit strange—out of the norm—and far from the quiet, retired-in-the-countryside life that many dream of for their later years. But for Glen and me, it is exactly what we have been praying for since our children were born. It's family and connection and love and God's mercy all rolled up into one messy package.

You see, I didn't have a close-knit, faith-filled family as a child. I had hard-working parents who put food on the table but rarely had time to talk to me or my siblings. As a child, I never had a true, deep, disciple-building connection with anyone. And I had no idea if connected family living was worthwhile or even possible.

But I knew I wanted something different for my kids' childhood. I wanted to break the cycle. I wanted to raise my kids so that they would leave my nest strong in their faith, with dreams to better their world, and so connected to family that they would be relentlessly drawn back to the very place where these foundations were formed. I wanted my family to have a spiritual heritage, to live connected, God-loving, and joyful lives.

I remember holding my eldest daughter, Erin, in the hospital after she was born. She was tightly wrapped in a hand-knit yellow afghan, and her tiny blue eyes were staring up at me. I prayed then that my daughter would grow up not only feeling loved by her family but also knowing that her God loved her more than she could even understand. I prayed that her faith would solidify, never waver, never falter, never dip. And I prayed that I would be able to form a connection with her that ran deep—honest, true, pure, and holy—a connection that would bring us both closer to Christ.

That prayer was definitely bold. Perhaps I asked for an impossibility, but I deeply wanted to see our kids grow up to not only walk closely with God but also remain closely connected with their family. I believe that prayerful, God-seeking parents should pursue such ideals with passion and grace as we raise our kids.

That's what this book is about—not how to become a perfect mom or dad or grandma all wrapped up with a pretty red bow, but instead how to raise kids who willingly and capably express their faith, who live sanctified lives, who stand against a world that is anything but God-seeking, and who maintain a healthy, loving connection with family that endures well past high school into adulthood.

I want to be clear right up front—there is no formula. I can no more guarantee that your kids will follow God and stay connected to you than I can guarantee you will take your next breath. I won't give you a list of things you must do or should do or even can't do. Instead, I'll give you a collection of ideas and advice from Glen and me and parents like us who have raised their kids and desperately want to show the next generation what a Christian heritage is. And I'll describe how you, in turn, can raise the next generation of Christian warriors, ready to do battle against a world that seems more desperate every day.

That's not to say my life has been perfect. There have been plenty of angry conversations and tearful prayers—times when I've wondered what went wrong. But there has also been much sharing of hearts over cups of coffee, and much time on my knees in prayer, and much forgiveness from everyone.

So it is that now I live within a few miles of all of my kids and grandkids and spend most Saturday mornings eating cinnamon rolls and drinking coffee around my crayon-covered kitchen table. Life is sweet—wild, messy, and sweet.

I pray that the words in this book will find you in similar circumstances twenty years from now—circumstances reachable through years of trial and error, and prayer—with strong families, beautiful marriages, and bright-eyed, Jesus-seeking kids.

And a kitchen that smells like cinnamon and has sticky handprints all over the table.

Part One

Creating an Atmosphere
for Spiritual Heritage

Chapter 1

The Generation Connection

Glen and Ellen

SOMETHING WAS WRONG WITH Sophie.

Her mom, Natalie, sensed this deep inside. Sophie had changed since starting eleventh grade. She had become sullen and secretive and refused to make eye contact. Natalie wondered if her daughter's behavior was caused by a bad influence in her new circle of friends or if perhaps it was an immature response to the independence that went with being allowed to drive. Natalie felt that Sophie's character had altered so much that she was no longer the young woman she had been raised to be.

Words jumped out from Facebook as Natalie passed by Sophie's open laptop lying on the dining room table. Worry compelled Natalie to continue reading the message thread, overriding the guilt she felt in breaching her teen daughter's privacy. Sophie had not even logged off Facebook or tried to hide the evidence. It was almost as if she wanted her mom to see what she was doing, a subconscious plea for help, hope that someone would grab her by the hand and drag her out of the mire before she sank too deep.

Natalie gripped the chair tightly and held back tears as the truth glared at her from the computer screen. Sophie had been sneaking out at night. And it was no longer just to visit friends or catch a movie, as she had done

one Friday night of her sophomore year. No, Sophie had gotten involved in much worse mischief than that.

"Our family Christmas trip will be such a drag. Nothing fun will happen at all," she had written. "At least you know how to have fun. I'll see you at Sam's on Saturday. As long as I can drag myself out of bed for church on Sunday, my parents will never know. I'll bring the weed. Don't forget to bring condoms. Wink, wink."

Natalie didn't want to read more, but she knew she had to if she was going to help Sophie. So she scrolled down. What came next broke her heart into a thousand pieces. There were messages about sex and parties and sneaking around written to and from Sophie's new boyfriend, Todd, whom Natalie had met only once, messages written to new friends who seemed to be nothing like her daughter's old friends, and messages with words that Natalie had hoped Sophie didn't even know, much less use.

Within minutes, it became clear that her daughter—the girl who had made a vow to remain pure just the year before—was not only having sex but also drinking and experimenting with drugs. And she no longer wanted anything to do with God or the lifestyle she had been trained in.

How could Sophie's life have changed so much in just a few short months? And how could Natalie help her daughter, who had walked so far away from how they had raised her? This story is a parent's worst nightmare, and there is no magic wand that will prevent your child from rebelling, but it is possible to raise kids who stay strong in their faith—kids who choose right, who stay connected, who love deeply, and who passionately pursue God. Yes, it is possible even in this topsy-turvy world where right and wrong are often difficult to define.

While God's plan for your kids is just that—God's plan—he often uses parents and their influence to build a spiritual heritage. He often uses parents who maintain a relationship with their kids far into adulthood that is connected, God-centered, and future-seeking.

Does that mean Sophie's parents have no hope? Absolutely not. God can redeem anyone. He holds our children in the palm of His hand, and we can trust Him to hold them tightly and pull them back to Him even when hope seems futile. The truly incredible thing is that many of the principles we'll show you to help prevent rebellion can also entice your children back to God.

So we want this book to serve as both inspiration and hope, as both help and encouragement, and as a way for you to see your family in a new light: as making a slow, prayer-fueled journey to a beautiful, God-centered heritage. A journey that, yes, will have many bumps and bruises along the way, but a journey that, in the end, will be remembered as a beautiful trek toward God's promise.

What *Heritage* Means

We are big believers in heritage. Especially spiritual heritage.

Perhaps it's because I (Ellen) didn't grow up in a household with a spiritual heritage. Sure, I had a heritage—a Finnish one—from which I learned the value of hard work and determination, and of curiosity and innovation. It was in our DNA as a Finnish family.

Yes, I had a heritage, but I did not have a *spiritual* heritage. My parents were more focused on their own lives and work than they were on raising kids to love God and live virtuous lives. I remember longing for more, and even vowing that I would give my kids more, but never knowing exactly how to make that happen.

Glen, on the other hand, was raised with a strong Christian heritage. His staunch German Baptist parents weren't perfect, but they understood heritage. They had morning devotions around the breakfast table (his mom made bacon *and* sausage every morning), they had Christmas tree hunts as a family, they swam in the local swimming hole every summer. They prayed together. They played together. They were together.

His parents certainly got it. A spiritual heritage is nearly impossible to define but is intuitive to understand. Creating a place where beliefs are handed down, a home in which children are viewed as a heritage of the Lord, makes sense to some people. Others have to fight for it but also manage to understand.

Heritage is connectedness.

It's vision.

It's the courage to stand up for what you believe in as a family.

It's the ability to say no to busyness and yes to tradition.

It's hope in Christ.

It's interdependency.

It's individualism defined within the context of family.

It's the result of much prayer.

It's love personified.

It's a capacity and willingness to forgive.

It's a choice to be a family that blesses others.

It's everything that God says in the Bible about family and parenting all thrown together into a messy, love-filled household.

And it's a key to raising kids who still stay connected to both God and family once they are out in the big, wide world. Parents who focus on developing a heritage with a strong spiritual component when their kids are being raised give their kids the tools they need to stay strong once they leave.

This is important. But it's also really hard to do.

The description of a spiritual heritage goes way beyond what we can say in this book, but we pray that this book will at least help you start building your family's heritage. We hope it will be a volume that you will refer back to for ideas, tips, thought-starters, and models for prayer.

Before we move on, let us confirm that in twenty years, you will, in fact, look back and regret some missed opportunities. Hindsight has twenty-twenty vision, and you will certainly think of ways you could have done things better. And this isn't a bad thing!

We firmly believe not only that you will likely get a second chance as grandparents, but also that it is downright impossible to make an unforgivable mistake that will destroy your family's heritage. God the Father just doesn't operate in the realm of unforgivable mistakes. You can't miss a step, miss your cue, have a bad day, and throw it all away. Instead, heritage is a twisting-turning journey with a path that goes through mountains and valleys and down the sides of ravines. One day you will be walking in a beautiful meadow, and the next day you'll be falling off a cliff.

But that doesn't mean you have failed. And it doesn't mean your kids are destined for failure. Quite the opposite. Those cliff-falling days (like the one Natalie had at the beginning of this chapter) are just reminders for us to buckle down and prayerfully trudge on, to keep building and defining a heritage for our families.

It's never too late. God loves you. He loves your kids. And He wants to give your family a spiritual heritage that will last for generations.

Start Your Family's Spiritual Heritage

Starting is easy.

Just turn to God—right here, right now—and say, "Lord, I want to be a heritage builder for my kids. I want them to value and remember special times we share as a family and practices we adhere to that unite our hearts and minds. But more than that, I want my kids to yearn for You so eagerly that they will be able to resist every temptation that the world would put before them. I want them to be so connected to me and to our family that they know they can turn to us with anything—any burden, any problem, any hope, any dream. I want them to love fully, to understand deeply, to connect wholly, and to seek you with every part of their beings. I want to give them a spiritual heritage that will grow and flourish for generations. Amen."

That was easy, right?

Now comes the hard part: you have to make cinnamon rolls—from scratch. We're kidding. (But we did put our recipe at the end of this book, if you are dying to try them. They are ooey, gooey delicious.)

In the coming chapters, we'll look at the next steps. The stories we've collected there are a little more rubber-meets-the-road. But without prayer, nothing else matters. So, seriously, go forth and prayerfully make a heritage for your family, because family is at the center of God's design and purpose.

And whether you have toddlers or teenagers or even college kids like

Sophie who have already drifted away, it's not too late. You can do this. And God will help you leave a heritage that will reach your kids, your grandkids, and your future descendants.

Quick Tips for Establishing a Spiritual Heritage

1. Share with your children and grandchildren your own journey of faith. Describe both the up times and the down times. Tell them of both the good and the bad decisions you made, as well as the outcomes of each.
2. Verbalize for each child individually your vision of them loving the Lord and serving Him with purpose.
3. Tell them of individuals who were inspirational to you and how they helped you grow.
4. Celebrate Christian holidays joyfully and reverently. Build traditions that help your kids and grandkids remember these holidays in special ways.
5. Read the Bible together as a family. Talk through the readings and apply them to your family's relationship with God and with each other.
6. Go on a mission trip together. By taking care of the spiritual and physical needs of others, you will strengthen your own family.
7. Make it a stated family aim to be a blessing to other families. Then put it into practice by scheduling times to serve those in need together as a family.
8. A spiritual heritage includes the past as well as the present and future. Help your kids and grandkids to understand where they came from. Share with them the history of their family.

In the very beginning, God commanded Adam and Eve "to leave" and to "hold fast" (Gen. 2:24) and to "be fruitful and multiply" (Gen. 9:7). This directive doesn't apply just in the physical sense—although it certainly means that God calls us to form physical families. God was also commanding Adam and Eve and all future families to multiply their spiritual heritage. Family is where children are most apt to learn what it means to be a citizen of God's kingdom and, as such, how to bless and serve the world around them. And family is the place where your children will learn what it means to be a child of God. That is why spiritual heritage is so important, and it is why we as parents and grandparents and even great-grandparents must intentionally and prayerfully build families that offer children a glimpse into God's own heart.

Chapter 2

The Balance Between Justice and Grace

Ellen

SEVERAL MONTHS AGO, A woman named Dawn asked me to coach her as a parent. She was at a loss for what to do for her struggling eleventh-grade son, Andrew, and a friend of a friend told her about my work as a one-on-one family discipline consultant.

I arrived at Dawn's house, and she answered the door with red eyes. She had clearly been crying. Her husband, Eric, stood behind her, grim, frazzled, and unshaven. They ushered me into the living room where Dawn began to sob.

Eric began. "My stepson is—he's just lost. We don't know where to turn." He showed me a picture of a dark-eyed boy wearing a University of Texas T-shirt, a kid who could be one of my grandkids in a few years—cute, happy, and so, so young. Eric continued to tell me Andrew's story, which started with his parents' divorce. Dawn's first husband had just up and left when Andrew was eight. Andrew loved his father deeply and immediately spiraled downward—desperately trying to understand why his father had walked out on them. Even after Dawn met Eric and they married, Andrew continued to struggle.

Emotions were overwhelming the family. Eric felt guilty because he wasn't able to be the father figure Andrew needed. Dawn felt guilty because her decisions had affected her son so negatively. And Andrew? He numbed his pain with drugs and alcohol. Dawn and Eric had tried everything.

Their pastor had suggested strict consequences, so they had grounded Andrew for a month, telling him he couldn't leave the house other than for school. That had ended with a knock on the door at two in the morning. Andrew had snuck out, stolen their car from the driveway, and gotten pulled over for driving under the influence and without a license. Dawn was just glad no one had been hurt by Andrew's recklessness.

A friend had suggested therapy, and they tried it. But Andrew had sat stoically in the counselor's office, refusing to share even a word.

Dawn and Eric had no idea what to do. They had already taken away every privilege Andrew could possibly have. They had put a lock on his bedroom door and window. He had no access to the car keys. He had no means to call friends. He had hours of chores. And yet Andrew seemed to be spiraling downward even more.

Dawn looked at me between sobs. "Ellen, he just doesn't have anything else I can take away from him. I can't be any stricter. He's just . . . hopeless."

My heart sank at her desperation—but not at Andrew's future, because after working with kids for more than forty years, I know one thing: no one is hopeless. My first words during that parent-coaching session probably caused Dawn and Eric to think I was crazy. They may sound crazy to you too. My first recommendation to Dawn and Eric was just the opposite of what everyone else was telling them.

I told them to give Andrew fewer restrictions. I told them to give him more love, and to show him a little bit of grace.

Dole Out Justice, Mercy, and Grace

I know this sounds counterintuitive, especially to those of us who have read all the Christian parenting books that pronounce again and again that obedience is key to raising good kids. But please hear me out.

It's not that obedience isn't important—the Bible is very clear that obedience leads to godliness—but the way we have been taught to deal with disobedience is often counterproductive.

God does not dole out strict consequences to us every time we disobey. Just imagine how oppressed we would feel if He did! What if God struck you with a consequence every time an angry thought crossed your mind? Or a sharp word left your tongue? Or an unprayerful moment entered your day unchecked? We would all be walking around with piles and piles of consequences and no hope for redemption. But God, in His infinite wisdom and mercy, doesn't deal with us that way.

Yes, at times, God deals out the justice that we deserve. He teaches us to obey His commands by reprimanding and holding us accountable. We sometimes suffer the consequences of our actions in very real ways, even as adults.

But other times, He gives us mercy. He outright forgives us and gently reminds us of what is right in a way that is so merciful and kind that we can't help but want to obey Him.

But there is more. God also deals with us with heaping doses of grace. He died for our sins when we were still sinners. He forgave us, wiped our slates clean, and gave us incomprehensible, indescribable grace—grace that causes our hearts to sing and our minds to seek Him and follow Him despite our wavering.

God deals with us using a perfect mixture of justice, mercy, and grace. This is our spiritual heritage in Him.

And yet often times as parents, we dole out justice and leave mercy and grace to God. It shouldn't be that way. We're tasked with implementing both justice and mercy. A spiritual heritage is incomplete unless both are wholly in play.

When my daughter Erin was little, I was just starting to contemplate this idea and how it applied to me as a mother. Erin was seven or eight, and she had been lying about brushing her teeth. One morning, I caught her in the act.

"Erin, did you brush your teeth?" I asked.

"Of course, Mom," she said, smiling widely as she ran out the door and went to school.

I went into her bathroom and found her toothbrush dry as a bone. She hadn't even turned on the faucet. I had all day to contemplate what to do. I could deal with her with justice—give her some extra chores or take away her TV privileges for lying, in hopes that she would remember not to lie the next time I asked her. I could give her mercy—tell her that I knew she had lied and remind her that lying is wrong but that I forgave her like God does. Or I could give her grace.

I decided to try grace. I went to the Christian bookstore and asked if there were any good kids' books about honesty. I picked one out, wrapped it, and left it on Erin's bed for when she got home from school.

She got home, found the present, and responded gleefully. She loved books and started reading right away. I didn't even mention the lying or the toothbrush. I just let her read and prayed that God would use this opportunity for me to show her a little glimpse of Him. And the plan worked. A few hours later, Erin came out of her room ready to talk.

"Hey, Mom," she started slowly. "Thanks for the book. I love it. But I have something to tell you."

Erin confessed that she had been lying about brushing her teeth. We had a great conversation that night about honesty and how important it is to God. We talked without anger and without frustration. And we talked about the toothbrush incident when neither of us was angry or upset, when we had both come to an understanding.

She never lied about brushing her teeth again. And our relationship was stronger than ever.

Now I'm not saying that every time your kid disobeys, you should buy him or her an ice-cream sundae, but I do think that as parents, we need to prayerfully consider how we deal with our kids' disobedience. And in some situations, that may mean not doling out strict consequences.

It may mean giving them grace.

Build Connection

Back to Andrew.

Dawn and Eric were in a tough situation. They couldn't exactly give Andrew grace without making him dangerous to himself and others. He'd driven under the influence of alcohol. He'd lied. He'd endangered others. They would've been remiss to give him back the car keys for another chance.

But that didn't mean they couldn't show Andrew some mercy and grace.

As we talked, I realized that Dawn and Eric had been hearing from many well-meaning people that her job as Andrew's mom was to show him what was right and what was wrong, providing increasingly severe consequences for failures. But there's much more to parenting than merely handing down consequences and doling out punishments. While these can be useful training tools, their effectiveness depends largely on the means used and on the children's feelings toward their parents as authority figures. Doling out severe consequences without a heart-to-heart connection will remove effective parental influence from the equation.

To me, building a spiritual heritage requires that parents establish effective influence—an influence that will allow you to speak into their lives for many years, an influence that will inspire the trust necessary to turn them toward you when they need you most. And to have this influence, you need to first have a heart-based connection with your kids.

This connection doesn't come from constantly doling out consequences, from spouting off what's right and wrong, or from nagging or preaching. It comes from listening while seeking to understand their reality and loving them in the midst of their struggles. Listening, understanding, and loving—that's connected parenting.

For Dawn and Eric, this meant more listening to Andrew and less preaching. Together, we came up with a plan.

"What does Andrew like to do?" I asked them.

Dawn bit her lip and looked at me. "When he was younger, he loved the University of Texas basketball team. He was always looking up scores and spouting off stats to us at the dinner table."

"That's perfect," I said. "That's where we are going to start."

We got online and ordered tickets to the next Longhorns game. It was on a Thursday night the following week. Dawn worried about it being a school night, about messing with their routine, but I reminded her that connection is more important than routine and heritage is more important than homework. They bought four tickets: one for Eric, one for Dawn, one for Andrew, and one for Andrew to give to a friend.

A friend, you ask? Yes, a friend. Part of connecting with your kids is connecting with the people your kids love. Even if you are worried about those people's influence.

I could tell Dawn and Eric were very skeptical of this plan, but I was sure it would work. It would not solve everything, but it would at least give them that initial connection. It was a step toward a heritage.

That evening, Dawn and Eric gave Andrew the UT tickets and told him that he could invite a friend. They also told him they would take him and his friend to dinner before the game and that he could choose the place. Andrew gave them a confused look and grabbed the tickets with a scowl.

They worried he wouldn't go. They worried the plan would backfire and that their son would be even more angry, more lost.

But they were wrong. They reported back to me that on Thursday after school, Andrew had put on his UT T-shirt and hopped in the car, giving them directions to his friend Ashley's house. They said Ashley and Andrew had chatted through dinner (virtually ignoring Dawn and Eric) and held hands during the game. But Dawn and Eric had seen a few smiles, a tiny remembrance of the boy Andrew had once been. And then the next morning, he had come out and eaten breakfast with the family. He had even said thanks for the tickets and asked what they thought of Ashley. These tiny things are so big when you think about Andrew's heart.

I reminded Dawn and Eric that this is a long process, a journey—not a one-event-solves-everything thing—but that in the end, it would be worth it. These little moments of grace, of mercy, and of hope could change their family.

I have now been working with Dawn and Eric for more than a year. I encouraged them to implement weekly lunch dates with Andrew where one of them picks him up from school and takes him for burgers during his lunch break. I encouraged them to invite Ashley over and get to know her as part of Andrew's life. I encouraged more basketball games, more family outings, a road trip, books, and games. I also encouraged them to have dinner as a family, to read the Bible together, to talk, to ask questions.

I encouraged connection. I encouraged grace.

Andrew has since graduated from high school and is looking at community college. He is still dating Ashley. Things aren't perfect. He has struggled with attitude, with grades, and with alcohol. He still has a long road ahead of him. But the sullenness is gone, and hope has been restored for Dawn and Eric because, regardless of the issues and the struggles, they now have connection with Andrew. They have influence. They know him. And he knows that they love him.

And that changes everything.

Live with Hope

I think the thing that I have learned most from Andrew's story is that we cannot give up on our kids, whether they are lying about brushing their teeth, bickering with their siblings, treating you with disrespect, or beginning self-destructive behavior. God holds them in the palm of His hand, and the Bible says He won't let go. So why are we so tempted to?

I know that Dawn and Eric were ready to give up on Andrew, to call him a bad egg, to assume he had no future and was too damaged to make a difference. People told them they needed to tighten up, to show him what was right and wrong, to hold firm, to establish their authority. Accordingly, Dawn and Eric felt that if Andrew was rebelling, they couldn't do kind things for him without endorsing his behavior. No one mentioned that they needed to establish a heart connection.

The basketball tickets were not a reward for his bad behavior—the consequences of no keys still existed (justice). Attending the game was an effort to communicate a desire to connect with him regardless of his behavior (mercy).

Dawn and Eric didn't need to pull Andrew away from the world—from his friends, his social system, his school—in order to pull him away from bad decisions. Instead, they needed to connect with him on a level that would allow them to contribute to his decision-making process. And what he did wasn't up to Dawn and Eric.

Andrew is still getting there—but I continue to encourage Dawn and Eric to empower him, to give him tools, to send him out, and then to trust him to make good decisions. This doesn't mean being reckless (for example, giving him the car keys); it means being slow to anger and quick to dole out mercy and grace.

As stated earlier, a spiritual heritage is built on a foundation of family—a place where justice, mercy, and grace abide together. Justice convicts and teaches our children God's unchanging standards. Mercy and grace build in hope and draw our children to the cross of Christ by addressing the guilt and shame that mistakes and failures bring on. Children who grow up in such an environment are more equipped to stand in truth while graciously and compassionately loving others.

Quick Tips for Maintaining Justice, Mercy, and Grace

1. When your child makes a poor decision, prayerfully consider whether the message you want to send will be best delivered using justice, mercy, or grace.

2. Find ways to spend quality time with your kids. This may mean family dinners, an evening walk, or staying up until midnight on a Saturday night. But find time. Time is needed to connect meaningfully so that you can determine what your child most needs.

3. Listen to your child. Vow to spend at least ten minutes every day just listening to your child talk without nagging or inserting your opinion. In this way you will get insights you would not otherwise gain.

4. Write your child encouraging, positive, hand-written letters filled with memories and reasons why you love him or her.
5. Set aside one night a week for a family tradition. Maybe it will be a game night or an all-you-can-eat pasta night or a movie night, but keep your tradition to spend time together.
6. Be quick to forgive.
7. Be willing to hold your child accountable for poor decisions and actions. The best lessons in life come by way of facing the mistakes we make.

Think back on the last few weeks with your child. My guess is that you will quickly think of a few times when your child needed justice—maybe there was a lie, a tantrum, a moment when they made a terrible choice. Justice is necessary—we live in a broken world and serve a just God. But I'm guessing there were other times when your child needed mercy—a moment of brokenness when a mistake was made, or an incident where emotions and tears got the better of a child—and while they may have deserved a consequence, you chose to be merciful instead. Other times your child may respond best to grace; they might be allowed to have a play date or to go to a movie, even though they did not live up to their end of the bargain. Were you able to find a balance in how you dealt with your child? Jesus was full of both grace and truth (John 1:14). He rarely exhibited one without the other. And you can do the same. With thoughtful consideration, your kids will gain a spiritual heritage filled with plenty of both truth and grace and will follow Christ's example.

Chapter 3

The RITE Approach

Ellen

WE'VE ALL HEARD THE catchphrase—at church from the pulpit, at small groups, at a hundred different Christian conventions, and on a hundred Facebook posts: "Speak the truth in love."

Speak the truth in love.

You've said it, too, haven't you? And so have I. But I'm starting to realize that we—myself included at times—don't necessarily understand what that means. We have a tendency to use the phrase as an excuse to point bony fingers of justice at those in need of a moment of truth. We do it, after all, because we love them. It's merciful not to let them continue in their sin. Right?

But Jesus—the one who spoke the truth in love in a perfect manner—never once spoke truth with fire and brimstone and interventions and rejection (well, except a little when He was speaking to the self-righteous religious leaders of the time). Instead, He consistently, lovingly connected with those who needed to hear the truth in a way that made them want to hear it from Him.

Think of the story of Jesus with the Samaritan woman at the well (which can be found in John 4, if you want to read it). The woman was clearly a sinner—she was an adulteress, having had sexual immorality in her life for many years. If she had been alive in our time, I can only imagine how some of us Christians would be treating her. Facebook posts and blog articles would be written to chronicle her infidelity. Friends would turn the other way. Churches would refuse to welcome her. Perhaps friends would intervene to tell her exactly what her sin is and ask her to repent.

But Jesus didn't do any of those things. Instead, He loved her. He accepted her. He treated her with mercy and grace. Later we read He spent two days with her people. He spoke truth into her life—not in a condemning, condescending way, but in a way that showed He loved and cared for her regardless of her sin or how messy her life got.

Jesus makes it clear that He does not want us to remain in our sin. His desire for our purity comes from having already accepted us. He loves us regardless. He just wants what's best for us.

This is especially important with our kids who are still learning what truth is. If we choose to lecture, yell, threaten, and condemn, we simply drive them away from us. Without mercy and grace to temper our justice, we lose the ability to speak into their lives and pass along a valuable heritage, because they simply don't feel loved by us. And when we lose that loving connection, they often step away from the truth we are desperately trying to teach them.

So given our broken world with our not-perfect kids and our not-perfect selves, how do we speak the truth in love—especially when it comes to our kids and tough discipline situations?

The RITE Plan

RITE is a strategy that I believe allows parents to speak the truth in a loving way, while maintaining the relationship and establishing (or reestablishing) a heart connection. It's a means by which to establish a balance between justice, mercy, and grace, even as you discipline or mentor your kids. This strategy is also proactive and must be girded by prayer. When parents raise up their kids keeping in mind these four areas of needs, their kids are far less vulnerable to being pulled down by the culture at large.

The RITE plan has four roles for parents that allow the parents and child to grow closer, maintain connection, speak truth, and move forward. Each role is represented by one letter in the acronym. Here's how it works.

Step 1: Relate

God created each of us with a need to belong—to belong to Him, to belong to a family, to belong to a group. When this need is not met, we grow insecure and try all sorts of coping methods. Teenagers and young adults often cope by building relationships with people they feel accept them no matter what. We have no influence without connection. A spiritual heritage begins with relationship just like our spiritual walk begins with God extending His gracious love toward us.

In the story of the Samaritan woman, Jesus goes out of His way to encounter her. It takes place in the heat of the day, and he's in "enemy" territory. Instead of seeking an acceptable shelter, He sits at the public well waiting to welcome a woman rejected by even the "dirty" Samaritans.

Jesus waited to establish a heart connection before speaking truth to the woman, and so must we. As you work through whatever issues your family is struggling with right now, always remember that connection comes first, regardless of the age of your child.

No one ever said it was easy, though. I know when I am angry or upset with my kids, the hardest thing to do is find a way to relate with them, especially when all you want to do is dig right in with a lecture about how they need to shape up. But by starting with relating to a child, you communicate that your relationship with them supersedes anything they can do, and that your heart connection matters even when they have made a mistake.

Step 2: Inspire

After you've connected—or reconnected—with your kid, your job is to inspire them with your vision for their life. This doesn't mean lecturing them on the things they "could have been" or "could be" if they just change this or that; it means inspiring them with the vision of what you think God sees in them—their spiritual heritage in Him. Let yourself get starry-eyed on their behalf regarding your hopes and dreams for them. Let them know that God has good plans for them, ones that will bring them fulfillment even if they have made mistakes. Remind them that even poor choices by the Samaritan woman did not prevent Jesus from giving her encouragement about her future. Such inspiration will ignite hope in their hearts about who they are to become in Christ and assure them that current circumstances need not limit their future. Tell your child something positive: that he is a compassionate, kind friend; that she was born to be a leader; that he has an intuitive sense of values; that she is honest and loyal; that God created her in His image to do great things.

Step 3: Teach

Here's where the "truth" part comes in "speak the truth in love." I often tell parents that a reachable heart becomes teachable. Now that you have done the hard work of relating and inspiring, you can begin to teach your child what the Bible says about whatever the issue is. Jesus certainly didn't pull punches when He spoke to the woman at the well, but He also never condemned her. Just as Jesus did, speak to your kids like equals. Infuse your words with hope. Show your kids that you care about them regardless of what has happened and that your love for them will be unwavering regardless of what may happen in the future.

Step 4: Equip

Teaching is about informing our kids' minds so that God can continue His good work in forming their character. Equipping is about helping them gain the skills needed to follow through with what they know to be right, the tools they need to move forward. One kid may need to gain confidence by having opportunities to face his fears. Another may need to learn how to walk away from a toxic friendship, one in which she is being manipulated by a bully. And another may need to learn how to resist temptation.

Equipping is about helping your child practice the skills that reflect the godly principles they have been taught. Having been shown that your love and Christ's love for them are consistent no matter what, they are far more likely to be open to your teaching and training—or equipping. In other words, they have reachable, thus teachable, hearts—and you've made a way to speak the truth in love.

RITE in Action When the Stakes Are Low

I advise parents to use this strategy with their younger kids as well as their teens, and with their steadfast kids along with those who have lost their way. Last month, Katie, a mom of three, called me and asked to meet as soon as possible. She was distressed about her seventh-grade son. Sensing fear in her voice, I scheduled a meeting that very day.

Katie began by bursting into tears and blurting out, "I am so tired of arguing with Cole. When I ask him to do something he does not feel like doing, he says awful things—that he hates me and doesn't want to live in our family."

I could tell that Katie was ashamed to admit Cole's disrespect. Glancing down, she told me that she was waking up every morning afraid of what he might say and how she might respond. Her face softened, however, when she spoke of sweet moments she had shared with him as a young child.

"But now I don't even want to be in the same room with him," she stated angrily. She told me that the day before she had told Cole he would not be playing in the evening soccer game because he hadn't finished his homework, and that he had stomped up to his room and slammed the door, knocking a picture off the wall. "I can't do this anymore. How do I parent this kid?" she asked.

It became clear to me that Katie had a habit of lecturing Cole and telling him what to do. She was attempting to direct him without first relating to him. I could understand why Cole would cringe at being treated like a young kid, and I wondered if he had learned to put up a wall of anger to keep his mom at bay. Distance, rather than connection, had grown up between them. I suggested she start with relating and inspiring before moving on to training and equipping. I wondered if, in the daily busyness of caring for her three active sons, she had failed to connect with her middle son, who might be feeling misunderstood by her and therefore angry.

Katie went home that day, determined to listen and see things from Cole's perspective. Rather than correct him, she affirmed him. Rather than point out mistakes, she talked about his strengths and how she saw God using him in the future. She ran up to me in the school's parking lot a few weeks later and joyfully told me how much better things had gotten between her and Cole. Simply by not jumping right into directing and training him (teaching/equipping), she encouraged him to be far more receptive to what she had to say.

As I worked with Katie, I realized that she had fallen into a trap that so many Christian parents fall into: believing the lie that behavior improvement trumps the gospel, that true justice is devoid of mercy and grace.

I don't blame Katie. Many Christian parents have come to believe that keeping our kids from straying and redirecting those who have strayed takes careful, strict discipline. I tend to disagree. As we've shown, mercy and grace are key to both prevention and redirection. Only through a careful, loving relationship that allows for a mixture of mercy, justice, and grace will we build the heart connection with our children that allows us to influence them to move away from sin and closer to Christ.

So Katie started with relating. She took Cole out for ice cream, and they talked. She inspired him with what she saw as his potential. She talked about how much she missed their heart connection. Then came the teaching. She talked about respect and kindness and compassion and empathy. And then came the equipping. She let him come up with ways he could respectfully approach her. She suggested that he go out for a run or play hoops when frustration was mounting. She encouraged him to pause when he felt like screaming—to count to ten, take deep breaths, or pray. She assured Cole that she was there to help him learn ways to deal with his anger, ways that he would be happier with as well.

It worked. Cole started to check his attitude, and Katie started to hope.

The disrespect diminished. And their relationship was restored. It sounds simple. I'm sure it sounds almost too simple. But I can promise you that it works, not because it's a step-by-step process, but because you are treating your children as Jesus treats them: with love, respect, and vision.

His is the perfect example of how to love, connect, and help your kids thrive.

RITE in Action When the Stakes Are High

Taylor was a straight-A student who went to the University of Texas (Hook 'em, Horns!) on an academic scholarship. She loved kids, music, and horses and had plans to become either an elementary school teacher or an equine therapist. Her parents, James and Sharon, said that she had grown up in the church, had never wavered in her faith, and had always been known as the girl who served others with a kind, compassionate heart.

About halfway into Taylor's first year at college, James and Sharon, who lived about two hours out of Austin, got a phone call from an old family friend who also had a daughter at the University of Texas. Their daughter had called them with an alarming rumor: Taylor was pregnant. Apparently, she had met a twenty-eight-year-old single dad named Jonathan at a restaurant downtown and was spending all her time at his apartment. She was skipping classes, missing church events, and spending every waking minute with him.

James and Sharon were devastated. Taylor had worked hard in high school to prepare for a great future, and her parents were sorely grieved that she was throwing it all away for a guy. So on the advice of a pastor from their church, James and Sharon decided to stage an intervention. They headed to Austin, and upon arrival, insisted that Taylor take a pregnancy test. Although the test showed negative, James and Sharon dragged Taylor back to her room and quoted Bible verses about sexual immorality at her. They told her why sexual sin was so damaging and claimed that she had destroyed her future. They demanded that she break up with the guy and promise that she would never see him again. They also demanded that she seek healing from her sin with the help of a counselor and that she sign a pledge statement saying she would never again have sex outside of marriage. Then they explained to her that because she wasn't acting like the girl they had raised, they were pulling all funding for her schooling until she met their conditions.

I think you can probably guess how that went over with Taylor.

James and Sharon were speaking the truth—the Bible quite clearly speaks against extramarital sex. I have since worked with James and Sharon for many months, have glimpsed their hearts, and believe that they truly were trying to be loving. They wanted to do the right thing to help Taylor, but they weren't acting as Jesus acted, and they both confess as much. They had quickly condemned their daughter. They had spoken down to her. And they had believed the lie that many other Christians have also believed: that in order to stop sin, we must hammer the truth into a child's head rather than love righteousness into a child's heart.

Taylor asked James and Sharon to leave her room, and then she locked the door behind them. She declined all their calls and didn't respond to any of their text messages. After the semester ended, James and Sharon got news that Taylor had not reenrolled in school but had instead moved in with her boyfriend. She was working as a waitress at a café in Austin and helping her boyfriend take care of his toddler son. Her boyfriend had reportedly quit his job and was spending his days playing video games while Taylor paid their rent and bills.

It was at this point that in desperation James and Sharon reached out to me. Sharon tells me now that she fully expected me to tell her to stand strong, that they were in the right, that they had spoken the truth and their daughter had rejected it. She expected me to tell her to hold onto truth and pray for their daughter and that there was nothing else they could do.

But that's not what I said at all. I have learned over the years that holding fast to a conflict without reigniting love can destroy relationships. And I knew that if Taylor was to have any hope of turning her life around, her parents needed to surround her with truth and love. I firmly believe that, for Taylor and children like her, hope lies in the gospel—not in an intervention, in tough love, or in behavior improvement. So James and Sharon and I went straight to the gospel and saw that we are all saved through grace by faith. Taylor had been disrespectful, rude, and rebellious and had broken hundreds of God's "rules," but she was fully forgiven and washed clean. She was still a child of the one true God. God had not given up on her. He still held her in the palm of His hand. He still sought reconciliation and redemption. He would fight for His daughter. He loved her. And that meant James and Sharon should love her too, unwaveringly, unassumingly, and unconditionally.

I told them about RITE, and together we came up with a plan for applying it to their relationship with Taylor, starting with their need to relate. Taylor had entirely severed her relationship with her parents after their misguided intervention. James and Sharon had to establish a heart connection with their daughter that would allow them to speak into her life. They had to earn her trust before she could know she could turn to them even when she was doing things that might disappoint them. And they had to show her that their love didn't waver when she made poor choices.

Restoring the relationship presented a challenge, but before they could expect to move forward, they had to find a way to do it. I suggested they start with a humble apology via email, telling her that they had made a mistake coming to her in that way and that they were sincerely sorry. I suggested that they tell her they regretted that decision every day, and that they acknowledge the embarrassment and pain they had caused her. Finally, I suggested that they ask for forgiveness.

Asking for forgiveness was super important, because at this point, Taylor still blamed them for the broken relationship and for having to leave school. As long as she was blaming them, she was less likely to see her own need to change. Breakthroughs happen on the tails of humility—especially when displayed by the parent.

I warned James and Sharon that it may take time for Taylor to respond but that they needed to persist in seeking her forgiveness and working to restore the relationship. And they did. They wrote the first email that night and sent a similar text message a week later. After the text message, they got a text back from Taylor. It said, "Thank you for reaching out and apologizing." It wasn't much, but it was a start to repairing that relationship.

The next piece of advice that I gave James and Sharon will probably surprise you. I recommended that they reach out and try to get to know Taylor's boyfriend. Now I know this advice is counterintuitive. We like to stay away from the people who influence our children negatively. But God asks us to treat our enemies kindly and show them His love in all situations.

I reminded them that Taylor could very well marry this guy. It might feel daunting to show kindness to him now, but by rejecting him, they were possibly also rejecting their daughter's future relationship and future children—every future connection she might feel secure about right then. And I suggested that they offer to take Taylor, her boyfriend, and her boyfriend's son out to dinner, that they include her boyfriend in family events and invitations, and that they treat him with kindness, respect, and love.

I know that reaching out lovingly under these circumstances sounds difficult. Many parents think that by initiating that connection they are saying they approve of their child's choices. But I think that is merely a rationalization for being hard-hearted. There is a better perspective. By showing God's love to the people your kids love—regardless of whether you trust or like them—you are showing love to your children. Friends are important to your kids, and how you treat them will matter a great deal. You need to treat your child's friends with kindness and respect, but you can do it in simple ways: invite your kid's friends to family game night, take them to dinner, buy movie tickets for them. Find ways to get to know them.

Next up, James and Sharon needed to inspire their daughter. I want to be very, very clear: you cannot start the inspire stage until your relationship is in a good place. If you jump into inspiring before you've repaired the relationship, your words will fall flat and you will cause more damage.

It took more than six months for James and Sharon to gain Taylor's forgiveness and get back her trust. During that time, they called her every week and listened as she filled them in. In turn, they kept her updated about family things. They drove to Austin often to take her to dinner, shopping, or to the movies, or just to hang out. They also invited her and her boyfriend and his son out to the ranch for a long weekend. And on each of these occasions, they kept the conversations almost superficial. It wasn't that they didn't want to talk on a deeper lever, but they could sense Taylor wasn't ready.

Then one night, Taylor called them. She was crying after a tough day at work, and as they listened, Sharon realized that it was time to move forward. She told Taylor of the great potential she saw in her, that she had always known her to be a compassionate, kind, and driven person, and that she knew God was going to use her for big things. She told Taylor that she saw her working with children and changing lives in a big way. And she told her that, although she had hit some bumps, she knew that God was still going to fulfill His purpose in her life.

While the relate step can take months and months, you might very well go through the rest of RITE in one conversation. Sharon inspired Taylor and then moved right into the teach step. She told Taylor that, while their so-called intervention had not been a good strategy, the message behind it was good and still relevant. And that message is that God knows what's best for us and her decisions to disregard Him were costly to her. Instead of infusing her words with condemnation and condescension like before, Sharon infused her words with hope. God always forgives. God always restores. God always redeems. And there is no sin that can ever keep us away from our God and Savior.

Taylor opened up more and confessed that she had been feeling lost and alone. She said she didn't know what to do because she wanted to come back to God but she didn't want to break up with her boyfriend. Sharon listened, encouraged, loved, and shared.

The next day Sharon called and asked me to consult with her one more time, this time to help her equip Taylor. This was the hardest part for James and Sharon because they really wanted to stage an intervention—to take care of everything on her behalf, fast. Sharon was tempted to tell Taylor to move out of her boyfriend's house and back onto the campus that day, and to quit her job too. But I reminded her that a plan like that could easily backfire and drive Taylor away again. At this stage in her life, Taylor needed to figure out for herself how to walk out of the mess she had gotten into. Their role was to equip and guide her, which they realized is more difficult with a child who no longer lives at home.

My first suggestion was to offer Taylor her tuition money back. James and Sharon had been impulsive when they said they wouldn't pay for her tuition if she was going to be promiscuous, and Taylor had rashly withdrawn from school. She had been a top student, earning high grades in all her classes, so I suggested to James and Sharon that, if they could afford it, they should make being a good student the only string attached to Taylor's tuition money. She wasn't living the lifestyle they wanted her to live, but the truth was, she had a greater chance of moving forward in her life if she returned to school and worked hard toward her degree.

James and Sharon did offer to provide Taylor with tuition money and living expenses, provided she reenroll at UT and continue to get good grades in her classes. And Taylor jumped at the opportunity. But James worried that, by giving her money for rent and food, they were encouraging her living arrangements and enabling her to support her boyfriend. He said to me, "By offering to support her, I'm basically telling her I condone her choices." And he had a point—it was a lot of money and there was a risk that she would misuse the funds. I can understand James's struggle.

But there is a flip side. Taylor is clearly a hardworking kid who is successful in school and at her job. By giving her access to a college degree, they would give Taylor the means to support herself, to move out on her own, and to build her own life away from her boyfriend. Basically, her education would eventually equip her to break up with him, or, at the very least, to jump-start her future career.

"But what if she doesn't break up with him?" Sharon asked.

I reminded her that it was possible that Taylor would never break up with him. Maybe she would marry him, but Taylor would likely get tired of being the only one working. And that meant her boyfriend would need to shape up or lose her.

I also reminded Sharon that this situation was an opportunity to speak into Jonathan's life. She could show him God's love. She could share the gospel with someone who clearly needed it. The truth is that he also is a son of the King who desperately needed some hope. I told her that she and James should be praying not that Taylor would break up with her boyfriend but that she would rediscover Christ's purpose for her life, and I noted that Christ's purpose could involve Jonathan.

Equipping is the hardest stage because parents often have to choose between letting the child gain skills independently and providing needed support. Taylor's parents struggled with how to help Taylor appropriately while still allowing her to strengthen and grow by learning through her choices and mistakes. Sometimes the decisions get really tough.

Recognizing where our kids need to grow is the key to success in any stage. For example, I see a dire need in girls who get caught up with "predator" boys to learn how to stand up for themselves—to learn how to lovingly confront others rather than just be nice. All their lives, they have been told to be nice and respectful, but that counsel has not equipped them to stand up to manipulation or to remain firm when being pressured. Helping them practice this skill before they leave home could serve as a strong preventive measure to getting manipulated into unhealthy relationships during their college years and beyond.

Likewise, I see a dire need for us to equip all our children with the skills to participate in healthy conflict. So many kids toss aside relationships because they don't know how to resolve arguments. In the equipping stage, we can equip our kids to pursue relationships truthfully and lovingly, as God does.

As a general rule of thumb, I suggest equipping your child in any way that leads toward a stronger future. Consider their strengths and abilities, and their weaknesses. Equip them by giving them opportunities to develop their talents and skills. As their competence grows, so will their confidence. Also guide them to overcome their weaknesses on their own. They all have areas in which they are weak, and if ignored, these weaknesses can hold them back. Here are a few examples:

- Give your quieter, even-tempered children the time to speak up and express their opinions. Often these kids are afraid or don't know how to express their feelings, and they need plenty of practice to gain the necessary skills. Your explosive, emotion-driven kids, on the other hand, need to gain the skill of thinking before reacting.

- Give your people-pleasers, those sweet children who don't want to disappoint you, plenty of opportunity to express their ideas without judgment so they learn how to say no when they need to, and stick to it. Let them know that their opinions matter to you and that you honestly want to hear what they're thinking even if it goes against what you think.

- If your child has a fight with a friend, talk him through it and give him strategies for finding ways to resolve conflict.

- If your child has a manipulative friend who threatens and bribes her, give her guidance on how to walk away from a toxic friendship.

- Let your kids struggle through their schoolwork without stepping in too much. Their confidence grows when they discover that they can face challenges and figure them out on their own.

- With your older kids, sit down and discuss job skills, college essay ideas, and application questions, but don't fill out their applications for them. Help your college-age child plan a budget on a spreadsheet, but don't hand over a large sum of money without accountability.

The RITE plan will help you maintain a balance of justice and mercy in your home, whether you have young kids trying to cross small boundaries or older kids crossing big ones. Because of its emphasis on relationship building, prayer, reconciliation, and redemption, the RITE plan can repair rifts with teenage or adult children and help them pull away from whatever trouble they have become involved in. There is nothing your child can do that will turn away their heavenly Father's love, and likewise, there is nothing your child can do that should turn away your love.

So get ready to prove it.

Quick Tips for Initiating RITE

1. Reach out with mercy. Justice punishes us for our errors, but mercy restores us to our former relationship.
2. Step forward with a hug. Make yourself a safe person for your kids to come to.
3. Instigate a conversation that will encourage healing. You may have to offer the first apology.
4. Offer forgiveness, just as Christ forgave you.
5. Share from your heart. Be authentic—that is, vulnerable and lovingly truthful, not tiptoeing around unpleasant facts.
6. Listen intently. Don't think about what you want or need to say next. Focus on your child. Listening attentively shows that you love and value your child.
7. Be willing to see the other side of the dispute. Remember that understanding what is going on with your child does not mean you agree with them.
8. And always, no matter what, no matter when, no matter what it takes, make your love unconditional so that Jesus shines through you.

Your child desperately needs to connect with you and God—especially when he or she is making poor choices. Kids need to know that their mistakes are not irreparable and that you hold out hope for them. When you extend mercy and express belief in your child when that child has done something wrong, his or her heart is more apt to soften. With a softened heart, your child will be willing to listen to what you have to say and more willing to do what is right.

Chapter 4

The Informing of a Mind

Glen

A SIGN ON THE door outside my office reads: Glen Schuknecht, Director of Discipline and Discipleship. Apart from making me seem very serious and directorial, this title means that I get to meet with students who have made poor choices and help them to find better choices.

Now I've been an educator for more than forty years, and I've learned that kids already know it all, or at least they think they do. This means that, even with all my fancy degrees and all my life experience, my words don't stand a chance—unless they are infused with more than knowledge.

Knowledge just isn't enough to convince kids to choose what is right.

Even Satan—who conspires to destroy all—knows what is right. When he tempts Jesus in the desert, as described in Luke 4, he actually quotes Psalm 91 to Jesus. He knows the Bible inside and out. He understands the earth and how it works. He knows God created the earth. He knows that God desires what is good, true, and beautiful for each of us. But knowing all of that does nothing if he has no desire to do what's right.

Likewise, our heads know what we should do, but our hearts, which happen to be sixteen inches away, can lead us astray. I like to call this the sixteen-inch miss. Kids know that it's a bad idea to cheat on a test, yet they quickly jot notes on their arms when a pop quiz is announced. And they know that they should ask permission to go to an R-rated movie, but they know the answer will be no, so they go without asking.

Last week, Erin (my eldest daughter) heard loud music emanating from her son Will's room. His nursery rhyme CD was playing at ear-splitting volume. She walked in and found the curtains drawn, lights flashing, and four-year-old Will standing on his bed dancing his heart out to "Mary Had a Little Lamb," the disco-tech version. He had created a disco dance party in his room.

Since Will didn't own a disco ball, Erin looked around to figure out how the lights were flashing in all different colors. And then she saw it. Her nice, new living room lamp had been brought upstairs, minus its shade, and refitted with the flashing disco bulb that Will had somehow found at the top of his closet.

I mean, really, who would buy a four-year-old a flashing disco bulb?

Okay, they were included in an amazing Black Friday sale at Lowe's. There are ten more sitting in ten more closets around Austin, as I thought each of my grandkids needed one—for obvious reasons.

Erin was fuming—her nice living room lamp looked nothing like the lamp she had purchased to decorate her living room. She sat down with Will and asked him what he had been thinking when he had "borrowed" her lamp.

"Mommy, I wasn't thinking! I just saw that special light bulb and knew I had to find a way to use it! So I just went downstairs and really quietly found a lamp, and I did it," Will said, looking her in the eye.

"But did you know it was wrong to take my lamp, Will?" Erin asked.

"Yes, Mommy, I did. But that bulb was so pretty that I couldn't resist!" He started to cry.

And so goes the ethical failures of millions of kids all around the globe: I wasn't thinking. I knew it was wrong. I just couldn't resist. That special disco bulb that Opa got me was just so pretty.

The point here is that, even if you don't have an awesome Opa buying your kids super awesome (read: tempting) things, your kids must choose between right and wrong all the time. And the question isn't whether they know what's right (I'll give you a hint: they probably do), but whether they will choose what's right.

So how do we teach our kids to desire what's right even when there are flashing red and blue disco light bulbs involved?

Fiery Faith in God

Many people struggle to understand the difference between wisdom and knowledge. You can help your kids and grandkids gain that foundational understanding by encouraging discussion on the subject. Solomon had a lot to say about wisdom and knowledge. To get things started, turn to the beginning of Proverbs and have a race to see who can find the first verse about wisdom—it shouldn't take long.

I grew up in a great home, except that my Dad was hypercritical. I could have gained such wisdom alongside the knowledge I received from him, but his criticism and my pride got in the way. He raised me with strong Christian values, but I often hid in my room, picking and choosing which knowledge I would allow to spark a fire in my heart.

I grew to have a ton of head knowledge about my Lord in early adulthood, but very little passion. I describe myself at that time as a big oak log. I was big and bulky, but I was wet and hard. Without kindling and paper, that log would not burn. I was solid but not on fire for God. In college, I led Young Life (a Christian youth program) and developed some mild evangelical warmth, but honestly, my life with Jesus lacked passion.

When Ellen and I got married, my lack of passion became a significant struggle. I knew I was failing as a spiritual leader. Then when the kids came along, leadership got harder still. I tend to shy away from things I can't or don't do well. It was tempting for me to skip relating and inspiring and move right into teaching—with a side of lecture.

But Ellen was on fire for God. My head knowledge, acquired through years and years of Christian influence, might have beat hers, but her passion outshone mine by miles. It is hard to lead from behind, so I simply went through the motions. I faked it. I loved being used by God on mission trips and in lunch-time Bible studies every Wednesday at the high school where I taught, but looking back, I'm not proud. I realize that God used a lukewarm believer.

Sadly, I think many of us guys fail in leading our wives and children. We want to lead in our own strength instead of letting God work through us. But God did use me. Isn't that interesting? Even when we are struggling and failing, He uses us.

And what's more, God (and my wife) never gave up on me.

I have never done a great job of leading Ellen. There were thousands of times when I knew what to do but shut down and did not lead. Ellen, however, has been gracious in my failure. I am amazed at the miracle of my life. I have a wife who loves me in spite of my weak leadership—and the fact that I'm bald. Adding to that, all three of my kids love the Lord and are raising their families in strong godly homes. What a blessing!

God gives me new knowledge, even at my age, about discipleship, marriage, and leadership. Ellen and I often get to share what we've learned through our church's premarital counseling ministry, and we also get to speak in marriage seminars. Some of my head knowledge has seeped into my heart over the years, and now when I occasionally fall into the trap of relying on head knowledge, verses like Psalm 63:1 or Psalm 84:2 pop into my head, and the Scripture sparks a fire in my heart.

Passion has made a huge difference.

Foundational Knowledge of God

I just told you that knowledge isn't enough to prevent your child from playing with tempting "disco light bulbs," like dishonesty, disrespect, envy, lust, unkindness, gossip, slander, or laziness.

Yes, knowledge isn't enough. But for our kids to truly desire to please God, they have to have a foundational understanding of who God is and what He stands for. How can they serve Him if they don't know Him?

Our goal for our kids (and ourselves) is such a profound understanding of God that they recognize Him in everything they see and such an intimate relationship with God that they hear God's voice and intuitively press into Him when they need Him most. Then they will desire what is right, not because they are following rules, because Mom or Dad said so, or because they might get in trouble, but because they love Him.

But that all starts with knowing Him.

Throughout the New Testament, the Greek word *ginosko* is used when describing knowing God. The word describes intimate knowledge of someone, not head knowledge. It implies such great intimacy that it was used to signify sex. The meaning would not apply, for example, to knowing the president, that is, knowing all about him but having no experience or shared intimacy with him. *Ginosko* is our goal and prayer when we are teaching our kids to know God, not just the facts about Him but relational knowledge.

Ginosko means so many different things for so many different kids. And it can look so different in different families. But one thing is consistent: God is. He is the same, no matter how your kids learn about Him. So I encourage you to press into God yourself and prayerfully come up with ways to teach your kids about Jesus. Pray that He will reveal to them who He is, how He made them, and what His plans are for their lives. The following are a few ways to guide your kids into essential knowledge about God.

Books (and Audiobooks)

I love books—especially books that reveal who God is and how He loves our kids. Nonfiction books like this one can be really helpful for gaining knowledge and understanding. Children's books reveal the world to our kids in ways that they can understand. And great novels allow us to read stories (remember, Jesus was the ultimate storyteller!) that give us a glimpse into how heroes feel, think, and react. Each of them should hold a place in your life and in your kids' lives.

If your kids are too young to read or don't like to read, that shouldn't stop them from getting to know stories about heroes of the faith who can serve as good character examples. Make it a habit, from infancy on, to read to your kids and to talk about the stories around the dinner table. Consider listening to audiobooks as you travel in the car together.

Of course, you're probably going to ask me to suggest some good books (I know that would be the first question I'd ask). Unfortunately, my answer has to be vague—there are millions of fantastic books out there for all ages. So ask around for recommendations and head to your local library to see what you can find. Search on Goodreads.com. That said, I will list a few of my personal favorites for all age groups to get you started:

- For toddlers and preschoolers (I got lots of help from my daughters for this category)
  The Jesus Storybook Bible by Sally Lloyd Jones
  A Picture of God by Joanne Marxhausen
  Bible Stories Painting Books by Juliet David and Simon Abbott
  3 in 1: A Picture of God by Joanne Marxhausen
  Just in Case You Ever Wonder by Max Lucado

- For grade schoolers
  The Action Bible by Doug Mauss and Sergio Cariello
  Imagination Station series by Marianne Herring and Paul McCusker
  Candle activity books by Juliet David
  Adventures in Odyssey by Focus on the Family (also available as audiobooks)
  The Oak Inside the Acorn by Max Lucado
  The Chronicles of Narnia by C. S. Lewis (How can you write a book list and not put this in there?)

- For middle schoolers
  The Action Bible by Doug Mauss and Sergio Cariello
  The Love Comes Softly series by Janette Oke (especially great for a kid studying the pioneer times)

The Kregel Bible Atlas by Tim Dowley (especially great for kids craving facts and information about biblical times)

Grace for the Moment by Max Lucado

Prayers That Changed History by Tricia Goyer

You Have a Brain by Dr. Ben Carson

The Hiding Place by Corrie ten Boom

- For high schoolers

  The HCSB Illustrator's Notetaking Bible by Holman Bible Staff

  The Case for Christ by Lee Strobel

  The Preacher's Bride by Jody Hedlund (especially great for kids studying European history or the Reformation)

  Rooms by James L. Rubart (great for kids exploring who they are and who they want to become)

- For adults

  My Utmost for His Highest by Oswald Chambers

  The Knowledge of the Holy by A. W. Tozer

  The Hiding Place by Corrie ten Boom

  Novels by great current and past novelists like C. S. Lewis, Francine Rivers, Julie Cantrell, Jody Hedlund, Olivia Newport, and Cynthia Ruchti

  Anything by Tim Keller

  The Power of Praying series by Stormie Omartian

  Every Man's Battle by Fred Stoeker (some books you and your son can read together)

  Free to Parent by Ellen Schuknecht (of course)

Family Devotional Time

My family gathered together around the breakfast table for devotional time every morning when I was growing up. My dad read to us an entry from *Our Daily Bread* and a corresponding passage of Scripture, and then we prayed together. I confess there were times my brother and I groaned about these meetings. We often wanted to get going with the day or skip breakfast and sleep a little bit later. But my parents were insistent, and we started the day off in the Word as a family.

While a breakfast devotional may not work for some families—what with school schedules and sports schedules and everything-going-on-at-once schedules—I would challenge you to come up with a time to sit down together three or four times a week for family devotionals. Use that time to delve into the Word together, to discuss what you've learned, and to pray for each other.

Church

I have been surprised by how often I hear family members tell me that they are "between churches" or "worshipping at home" or "loving God but not His church." I think I understand why they stay away from church. Getting to church can be hard. First of all, extra time in a warm bed and a hot cup of tea really sound nice on a Sunday morning. Further, the church is full of imperfect people who make mistakes, don't lead well, make bad decisions, and don't honor God with their words or lives. People like you and me.

But church is important. The Bible doesn't say, "Thou shalt go to church every Sunday or thou shalt be condemned," but it does say we should seek to know God intimately (Ps. 63:1) and that we should not neglect meeting together (Heb. 10:25). Worshipping and praising God with a community of believers and learning about Him and His Word together is a wise practice. While it may be hard to refrain from hitting the snooze button, getting to church every week will satisfy even greater needs.

Before I move on let me add that I know special circumstances arise. Your kids get sick. You have a soccer tournament that lasts all weekend. You move and take some time to prayerfully find a new church. I'm certainly not saying that you must be in church every Sunday no matter what. I'm simply saying that your family should be connected to a church body and that your kids should see you sacrificially making it a priority.

Talking to Your Kids About God

In school, a couple of my grandkids work on exercises from the books *What Your Kindergartener Needs to Know* and *What Your Third Grader Needs to Know*, two of eight offerings in the Core Knowledge series. The pages are filled with fairy tales and anecdotes and excerpts from old literature and rhymes and songs—a wonderful mix of content that the authors knew would inspire kids of those age groups.

There is a book like that about God—the Bible, obviously—and the pages are filled with a wonderful mix of content that God knew would inspire each of us. What if we used the Bible as a guide—beginning early on—to teach our kids about God? To answer the hard questions? To help our kids grow in their knowledge of what is good, true, and beautiful? To teach our kids to rely on His strength in their weakness? To find models of what it means to be truly intimate with God?

Talking to your kids about God starts with conversation. It's inviting Him into your everyday experiences. Pointing out His creation in nature. Expressing gratitude. Praying. Acquainting your kids with Jesus is your greatest parental calling, so look for opportunities to converse about Him every day.

Quick Tips for Starting Conversation

To help you talk with your kids, I have prepared a list of major spiritual topics. I hope these topics serve as good starting places for ongoing spiritual conversation in your home and help to lay a foundation of intimacy with God for your children.

I. Who God Is
- Discuss the attributes of God: He never changes (Heb. 13:8). He is patient (2 Peter 3:9). He is righteous and just (Ps. 89:14). He is sovereign (Ps. 135:6). He is truth (John 14:6). He is love (1 John 4:8).
- Discuss God's redemption of mankind—His sacrificial gift to us to save us from our sin.

- Talk about God's eternal plan for us. Explain examples of how He works out His plan for us through the good and the bad events of our lives. Ask how knowing about His plan changes the way we look at our circumstances.
- Talk about God's prescribed principles. The Golden Rule (Matt. 7:12), for example, is the principle above all principles. It alone could govern relationships effectively.

2. Who We Are

- We are fearfully and wonderfully made, according to Psalm 139. Ask how that fact affects our choices.
- Our weaknesses and our strengths help us to glorify God. Ask how our weaknesses teach us to depend on Him. Ask how our strengths teach us to shine for Him.
- Each of our personal stories is observable in relation to God's story of redemption for all people. Ask how His redemption is playing out in our lives.
- Our family values come directly from God's principles. Ask what those important values are (honesty, integrity, courage, compassion, love, kindness, etc.).

3. Where We Are Headed

- Discuss how our actions line up with God's principles and our family values, and in which ways we need to alter our course.
- Ask what we can do to let a lost world see God in us. Ask who in God's kingdom we envision ourselves becoming.
- Talk about how we can do better at living with eternity in mind.

These are long, ongoing, important conversations that every family should enter into. So why not get started? Choose one of the conversation points above. Talk about it with the kids. Discuss different perspectives on it. Ask leading questions. Listen to what they have to say. Find illustrations that help them understand. And invest time in solidifying their knowledge of God.

The foundational knowledge about God that we impart to our kids when they are young becomes the basis for their adult faith. The Bible stories, those Sundays in church, those conversations about what's right, what's wrong, and what's crazy in the world—all contribute significantly to raising up the next generation of believers. That's why I take my job at the school very seriously. I want every single conversation I have with a child—however seemingly minor or insignificant—to help them understand who God is. Through us parents and teachers, God is laying the groundwork for a life-changing, fulfilling, and world-moving faith.

Chapter 5

The Boundaries That Connect

Ellen

As a child and adolescent, I experienced reoccurring nightmares. The dream was the same each time. I would be sitting in the front passenger seat of a car that was going along a narrow mountain road. Suddenly, at an unprotected corner, the car would career off the road and plunge down through air and trees into a deep canyon. Each time I dreamed the dream, I woke up as the car fell through the air, with my heart pounding.

Even now, as I write about this dream, I feel the panicky feeling well up in my gut. My heart still pounds. My palms grow sweaty. It's still a trigger for me, even fifty years after I started having that dream. And even more interestingly, after much prayer about it, this dream has come to represent my feelings and ideals about boundaries.

Let me explain.

I grew up out in the country with miles and miles of woods and fields around our homestead. We were given few, if any, boundaries with regard to what we could do in our free time. I shudder to think of how *freely* I grew up. As long as we were not interfering with my parents' work, we could do whatever we wanted. We forged trails several miles long through the thick wooded hills to our friends' homes. We climbed to the tops of the tall, very tall, evergreen trees. We rode old bikes along a winding, hilly country road (without helmets) to the nearest pool, which was ten miles away. We explored old abandoned shacks that were considered haunted. We spent nights by a creek that ran through our property, miles away from our home. We swam in the swiftly moving Columbia River without adult supervision.

We did things that most parents these days—for good reason—would never allow their kids to do. And this was both good and bad. I grew up feeling competent to take care of myself as a result of the freedom I had been granted, and I held myself responsible for paving my own way. I knew I was able to make good choices. I knew I was able to solve problems. And I knew I could face whatever came my way.

At the same time, without any boundaries, I felt insecure. Unprotected. I remember wanting my parents to say no to me at times. I wanted them to think about my safety, to worry about where I was and what I was getting into. The ten-mile bike ride to and from the pool was worth the effort because I loved to swim. But deep inside it frightened me, and even as a child, I wondered about the wisdom of taking this trek alone along a wooded, winding, hilly road. Later, as a fifteen-year-old, I secretly longed for them to stop me from dating a guy nearly five years older than me. I knew deep down that he wasn't a safe person and wasn't good for me. But they didn't seem to care. They continued to let me run my own life and form my own boundaries at an age when my discernment, as well as my ability to stand firmly for my principles, was not yet fully formed.

I believe this reoccurring dream represented these deep-seated feelings of insecurity that rose up within me as a result of having no boundaries. I longed for the security that wise guidelines and articulated values would provide me—guardrails along the edge of the road to halt my bike from careening off sharp curves in the road. I longed for someone who would worry about me enough to stop me from making mistakes, someone who would say no to me—and then yes. Boundaries would have been very healthy for me.

They are healthy for your kids too, which is why one of the pillars in my parent coaching business is to help parents as they establish healthy, connection-building boundaries with their kids. I help parents set boundaries that will stop the free fall while helping kids grow up as independent, brave problem-solvers.

Preconceived Notions About Boundaries

If you were raised under very rigid, rule-bound parenting, you may shudder at the word *boundaries*. Your own parenting tendencies may be a reaction to that upbringing, and you may be trying your hardest to be relational and not demand strict obedience. The boundaries I'm suggesting, however— the ones that kids crave, adults need, and God requires—are boundaries that actually *connect* parents and kids. They address the true needs of children as well as the desires parents have for their sons and daughters. This type of boundary allows you to carry out the RITE plan by establishing necessary standards, yet it gives your kids room to grow and learn.

Boundaries put in place simply for the sake of having rules in your household are anything but helpful. Boundaries that are listed by some expert, that are preached from the pulpit without an understanding of the situation, that exist without loving connection and a scriptural basis are damaging to your kids. And likely, your kids will reject them.

To a child who feels misunderstood and disconnected, boundaries will merely represent a line to cross. I want to be really cautious in how I address the topic of boundaries. I do believe that every one of us was born with a sin nature and that a time will arrive in each of our lives when we will want to cross boundaries, because, well, we are sinners. But I also want to say that it's not always the case. I do believe that for many children, the crossing of boundaries is instead a plea for connection. They want to relate to you, and for you to relate to them. And in their effort to get your attention—and connection—boundaries are crossed.

So I ask all of you moms and dads who grew up in the "era of unhealthy boundaries" to throw your preconceived notions about boundaries aside and willingly consider something new for your family, that is, a set of guidelines that connects you to each other and to God and an ongoing conversation that allows your kids to feel secure in knowing that someone is pouring their wisdom, protection, and love into them.

Boundaries That Promote Learning and Growth

The right boundaries give children room to wiggle and grow and try things out—to learn and to develop their own self-control and ability to choose well—but they put guardrails in place so that the kids don't fly off the path. When it comes to establishing boundaries, many parents simply pull out a ballpoint pen and write a list of rules for their kids, such as the following:

You will have a ten o'clock curfew.
You must do all your chores before leaving for school.
Your skirt must cover your knees.
You must not wear leggings in place of pants.
Your shirt must cover your backside.
Your hat must be on forward.
Your pants must be worn at your waist.
You must save 10 percent of your money for a tithe.
You must not smoke or drink or go out with those who do.
You must not take your phone into your room.

And all of these rules are fine—but outside of connection, outside of conversation, your kids will likely resent them. And then they will find ways around them. So I encourage you to start a conversation about boundaries with your spouse and with your kids—instead of writing out a list of rules. Here are a few guidelines I have for creating boundaries that connect.

Design Boundaries Specifically for Each Child

My two eldest children tended to be very social. In fact, if given the choice between studying and, say, going to FroYo with their friends, both of them would have chosen FroYo every time. And so with them, we had a household rule that the only weekday activities they could participate in were those related to school and church. Otherwise, they were to stay home on weekdays and spend time with family, preparing for the next school day, and getting a good night's sleep.

However, we changed this rule for our youngest. Alisa was a driven, perfectionistic teenager. Even if she had completely finished an assignment and checked it, she would have chosen to recheck it again and again to make sure it was perfect rather than do something fun. I remember finals week when she was in tenth grade. She had done so well the entire semester that, by our calculations, she could have scored only 50 percent on her final exam and still achieved an A in her geometry class.

We told her to blow the test off—just to do her best and not worry about the grade. Yet when her cousin who was visiting from out of town asked her to go to the mall, I heard her say no. Ten minutes later, I found her at her desk in her room, poring over her geometry notes. We made her go. Yes, we were those parents, the ones who made their daughter go to the mall rather than study.

After that, we made a new rule especially for her. Once she had finished her homework and checked it once, she was allowed to go out with friends—even on school nights—as long as she cleared it with us first.

You should have certain boundaries or house rules that apply to all your kids, but I encourage you to consider how each boundary applies to each of your kids, with their unique skills, gifts, and personality in mind. This is a means by which to relate uniquely to each child. Here are a few anecdotes to give you some more examples:

- My ten-year-old grandson, Joey, tends to lose track of time when playing video games on his Kindle Fire. He has been caught multiple times playing for much longer than the screen time he had been allotted. Because of his inattentiveness to time, he needs tighter monitoring in place when he uses devices than does his eight-year-old sister, Kate, who rarely plays games and would almost always prefer to color or play outside.

- My five-year-old grandson, Will, tends to be fearless. He will climb to the top of the tallest tree, stand on the highest rail on the swing set without holding on, and ride full speed down the hill on his scooter. Because of his recklessness, he needs closer monitoring when he plays outside than my four-year-old grandson, Asa, who tends to be more cautious and discerning.
- My seven-year-old granddaughter, Haddie, and my eight-year-old granddaughter, Kate, both tend to be messy in their rooms, closets, and backpacks. Because of their untidy tendencies, they both need more guidance and structure for staying organized than Joey, who naturally keeps his things in place.

In each of the above situations, a general rule for all the kids would be inappropriately stifling for those who don't need that particular guidance and improperly liberating for those who do. Joey, for instance, would be annoyed by a checklist for putting away his things every day, but Kate would be helped. Asa would probably never ride his scooter if required to check with his mother first. Will, however, would ride his scooter down a steep hill and into traffic without this check in place. By taking into consideration each child's unique personality as you establish boundaries, you are telling them that you understand who they are and that you believe in who they are becoming.

Agree upon Boundaries in a United Fashion

You are the parent. Your kid is the child. And you've probably been told one hundred and one times that you aren't your child's friend and that it's your job to set boundaries that will help your child become a responsible adult. And this is right . . . to a point.

Allowing your children to have a say in the boundaries you set doesn't make you any less the parent, and doesn't make them any less responsible. In fact, I would venture that the opposite happens. Involving your child in making boundaries allows you to lovingly connect with him or her, and it enables your child to gain important skills. It also provides a great opportunity to inspire them to think about how their decisions can affect their lives.

When our kids were teenagers, we never set a curfew for them. We felt that there were some situations where we would want them to be home by seven and others where we could confidently let them stay out until midnight. So instead of a curfew, our rule was that they come to us on any given night and tell us where they were going, who they were going with, and what time they proposed to come home. We then decided together if their proposal was appropriate.

One time my eldest daughter, Erin, was asked out by a football quarterback two years older than her. He wanted to go to a late movie and then for ice cream afterward. After a long conversation, we agreed on a daytime double date to the ice-skating rink with her friend. Erin was part of the conversation, so she never felt we were laying down overly strict rules for her.

On the other hand, when my youngest daughter went to prom her senior year with the boy she had been dating for three years, the kid whom my husband had mentored for hours and hours throughout high school, the man whom she would eventually marry, we happily acquiesced to her request to stay out until midnight so they could go get coffee after the dance.

Expect to Break Boundaries

I'm not saying kids should break the boundaries that you have carefully set in place; I'm saying instead that you should remove or loosen the boundaries once a child displays appropriate, responsible behavior. Basically, if they earn your trust, you show them that you trust them. Kids need lots of practice in making wise choices on their own while they are still at home and can come to you for help. This is equipping them for greater and greater challenges. And they need the freedom and independence to learn to make these decisions on their own.

We had two family vehicles when Erin got her driver's license. We didn't buy her a car—mostly because we didn't have the money but also because we wanted her to show us she was trustworthy first. We occasionally gave her access to the family cars, provided she gave us details of her plans. We wanted to know where she was going and that she wouldn't go far from home. We also wanted to know that she would be home at an early hour.

Erin followed these rules, for the most part, so we slowly began loosening our boundaries. We allowed her to stay out later, to go farther, and to pick up friends on the way to school. The more she showed us we could trust her, the more freedom we gave her. Eventually, we bought a third car. Technically, it was our car—we had the title in our names and safely stored in our lockbox—but she gradually earned freedom akin to that of ownership. She was allowed to drive a car that no one else drove, to go places even when Glen and I were using cars, and to store her stuff in the trunk. (Yes, the trunk replaced her locker and closet, and she could hardly get it closed.)

Similarly, we were pretty strict about the rules for slumber parties when the kids were younger. We allowed our kids to go to slumber parties only if we knew the parents well and knew they would be home while our kids were there. But by the end of high school, we relaxed those boundaries to allow our kids to make wise decisions on their own.

One night after Erin's senior year in high school, she wanted to spend the night at a girlfriend's house while her parents were out of town. A group of girls had plans to watch movies, eat popcorn, and talk. We weren't really thrilled with the idea, but we trusted Erin. It was time to trust her choices.

We said that she could go, but I reminded her that she was welcome to come home at any time in the night if she was uncomfortable. I also reminded her that while watching movies and eating popcorn was certainly safe, heading into town or inviting others over wasn't. Erin nodded and left.

Around midnight, I heard Erin's car in the driveway. Some of the other girls had decided to head into Denny's for pie with some guys. Erin had felt a little niggling of conscience about the idea, so she had decided to come home. We talked long into the night about this decision—and by the next morning we were happily chatting as we made pancakes together.

I had connected with my daughter because I had trusted her. And my daughter had proven she was trustworthy and equipped to handle an uncomfortable social situation. I imagine had we treated Erin differently—had we told her she couldn't go or had we put strict rules in place—she would have responded differently, certainly with anger. She may, possibly, have sneaked out. By loosening the boundaries, we tightened our connection. And we allowed our daughter to grow.

I believe that all—okay, most—boundaries for kids should be put in place with the intention of loosening them later. And by the time they go off to college—well, they shouldn't have any boundaries at all, from you, at least. The hope is that by the time they leave home they will have their own boundaries in place and be able to make great, wise, God-centered decisions without your help.

For his first year, my son-in-law attended a conservative Christian college that had all sorts of rules in place. He told me that one afternoon when he was studying in the student lounge, a girl from one of his classes asked him a question about an assignment. He responded by pointing out a passage in her book, leaning over to show her where the answer could be found. He says he spoke maybe ten words to her before the monitors ran to them, pulled them apart, and issued them several demerits. They both had to work on campus for hours to make up for their "infraction," and they were warned to stay at least three feet away from the opposite sex at all times.

It sounds like a police state under the guise of a Christian university to me. What exactly does a rule about talking to the opposite sex do? It certainly doesn't help kids follow a moral standard. Such rules are legalistic and unloving. Instead, the Bible tells us to love and honor others, to abhor evil, and to hold to what is good (Rom. 12:9–10).

I'll just say it: I think boundaries like those at that college are the exact opposite of what God calls us to impose on our youth. Such boundaries are not only damaging to kids' confidence but they are also damaging to their spiritual growth. At this age, kids need practice in holding to what is good in the face of temptation.

By the time our kids are ready for college, they should be equipped to make wise decisions on their own, not just follow rules. They should have the necessary wisdom because they have learned right from wrong and because God speaks to them directly. Whether our kids go to a huge secular university with few restrictions or to a small, private Christian college with strict boundaries, it really shouldn't matter because the truth should be written on their hearts.

Give your kids a chance to prove that you can trust them. Loosen or lift their restrictions and let them show you that they can make wise decisions. If they can't handle the responsibility, tighten up your boundaries again until you are ready to give them another chance to prove themselves. Be reasonable with how long you make them wait, however. The goal here is to give them plenty of time and space to learn to make their own decisions while they are still living at home.

And pray for your kids while they're learning.

Align Boundaries with the Real World

The most common questions I get asked by parents are questions about boundaries surrounding the use of computer devices and Internet technology. How old should my kid be before he gets a cell phone? How much screen time is too much? Should I let my kids play video games? What programs should I put in place to keep my kids safe online?

Questions such as these are really important because computers and Internet technology play a huge role in our lives. We use them to communicate, to play, to entertain, and to connect. And our kids may get into trouble using them. The extensive list of Internet traps is pretty scary: pornography, R-rated movies, cyberbullies, and predators.

My answer may surprise you: Your boundaries regarding technology have to align with the real world.

We live in a technology-driven world. Our public elementary schools integrate computers and tablets into the classroom. Our kids will use cell phones at some point. They will have computers in their dorm rooms and houses. They will have twenty-four-hour access to the Internet via tablets and mobile devices. Our kids are surrounded by technology.

So we need to put boundaries in place, not to restrict their use of technology but to teach them how to use it wisely. The boundaries you set should probably not attempt to restrict usage, as in "no cell phone until you are sixteen" or "no R-rated movies until you are eighteen." Instead, they should empower your kids to use technology wisely and teach them to restrict their own exposure.

For example, we held to a rule about the movies our kids could watch. When they were little, we allowed them to watch Disney Channel movies that we had recorded on the VCR, or nothing. But as they grew, we changed that boundary. Instead of saying no PG-13 or R-rated movies, we said, "Let's talk about any movies you want to see before you go see them." Yes, there were times we let them watch PG-13 and even R-rated movies before they left home. Our kids discussed their movie choices with us before carefully making their decisions. We asked questions such as these: Do you know that there is a lot of violence in that movie? Will that make it hard for you to sleep? And I heard there is an inappropriate relationship between the two main characters. How will that cause you to look at relationships?

There were times we let our kids go see movies that were perhaps contrary to our core values. We didn't allow them to watch pornography, of course, but some movies we allowed addressed topics in ways that opposed our beliefs. Oftentimes we went to the cinema with them. And always we peppered the drive-home conversation with truth and goodness and values. This growth-bringing conversation helped the kids see the world for what it is—a broken place—but it also gave them a good concept of the types of movies that they like and dislike.

Had our rules forbidden worldly movies, we would never have had those conversations. We may never have had the opportunity to address tough topics that our kids likely encountered at school, in the neighborhood, or later in the workplace.

I have a similar rule with cell phones. At least once a week, I have a parent tell me that they aren't allowing their kids to have cell phones until they are sixteen or until they can drive or until . . . whatever the case may be. I always ask them why.

And often the answer is something like "because kids shouldn't have phones" or "kids can't be responsible on phones."

I beg to differ. While I certainly don't think an eight-year-old is ready for a phone, I do think that, depending on your kids' maturity levels and individual needs, you should consider getting them phones when your family starts to need them for communication. For example, my ten-year-old grandson, Joey, plays soccer and often gets dropped off at practice for an hour or two and picked up later. My daughter was finding it difficult to know when she should go pick him up and where he would be. So she started giving him a phone—in this case, a family phone—to text her when and where he needed to be picked up.

Joey is ten, so he has strict guidelines in place. I think that is so important. He's allowed to text or call only his mom, dad, or grandma. He may not use the Internet. He may not play video games. He may not text friends. He may not download apps. My daughter is able to connect with her son when he needs her. But more importantly, Joey's learning good boundaries when it comes to technology. He's learning cell phone etiquette (for example, when texting an adult, you need to spell out full words and not use twenty emojis) and cell phone boundaries (no, his friends can't use the phone to really quickly call someone), and cell phone pitfalls (put the cell phone in a safe place before, say, jumping into the pool). By the time Joey is sixteen, he should have a good handle on how to use a cell phone correctly; that is, who to text when, how to use apps, and how to keep an expensive phone safe.

If we don't expose our kids to technology with gradually relaxing boundaries at an early age, we lose out on important opportunities to guide them toward wise, responsible use of technology, which likely will be a big part of their world.

So my advice to parents on tech boundaries is simple: Give your kids real-world exposure. Talk about the problems with technology often. Ask questions. Give your kids more freedom when they prove you can trust them. Take away that freedom when they prove that you can't.

And communicate, communicate, communicate.

Apply Boundaries to Everyone

Here's an interesting truth that may make you feel a bit squeamish: the boundaries you set for your kids should in some ways apply to you as well.

I know what you are thinking: You are an adult. You can do all kinds of things that your kids aren't allowed to do. Have sex. Stay up late. Spend money on that totally adorable pair of boots that you have been wanting for six months. And you are right. But the truth is, all the things that you do as an adult you do within boundaries. Boundaries reflect the values you consider most important, and they serve to unite your family. So any boundary that you set in place for your kids should in some measure also apply to you. Besides, you teach most effectively by what you model in your own life.

So does this mean you should set yourself a curfew? Absolutely not. But you should set family boundaries that are appropriate for all ages and that reflect your value system. Here are a few examples:

- Our family values a Sabbath, a day of rest, on Sunday. We also value going to church every Sunday as a family. It also means our kids were expected to attend a church near campus when they went away to college.
- Our family values modesty and respect. That means mom doesn't wear a skimpy bikini to the pool, and kids don't wear skimpy bikinis to the pool.
- Our family values edifying and uplifting language. That means that if you can't say something nice, well, you know the rule.
- Our family values family relationships over friend relationships. That means we treat each other well or don't get time with friends.
- Our family values God's plans for a happy and satisfying marriage.

That means we interact with members of the opposite sex with respect and reserve sex for marriage.

- Our family values good health as a way of honoring God. That means we get enough rest, eat healthily, and exercise regularly.

Toss Out the Rules; Pick Up the Grace

If I had to summarize this chapter in one sentence, I would say: toss out all the family rules you have in place, then work with your family to come up with a grace-filled set of boundaries that will help your family feel the freedom they need to follow God and make good decisions.

Quick Tips for Replacing Rules with Boundaries

1. Don't make rules or get rid of rules without a conversation with the kids involved. Their ideas will often surprise and delight you, and this is an opportunity to relate to and connect with them.

2. Don't have conversations without giving the context. In other words, make sure you clearly articulate the value of any boundary you establish, as well as your expectations for your children, and you will inspire them to aim higher.

3. Don't give the context without planning for grace. To be sure, your children will test the boundaries by bumping up against them, and even plowing through them at times. Boundaries help define standards for behavior, which your children need to know, but they will also need grace to encourage and motivate them to keep growing. Always keep in mind that the purpose of boundaries is personal growth, and you'll have opportunities to teach and equip your kids.

Let grace flow through every decision you make. Even when you have to tighten a boundary or let your child deal with the consequences of poor choices, be gracious. Don't lecture. And don't make empty threats, such as, "I will never let you drive again."

Getting rid of rules and replacing them with boundaries may make you feel like you are letting go of some of your parental control, and you are right. But you are exchanging control for something much better: your kids' ability to manage themselves—their self-control. As you let go of rules and boundaries that can actually stifle your kids' faith, you are giving your kids something far more valuable: the ability to choose right—to choose Jesus—because they want to, not because they have to.

Part Two

Choosing and Implementing Heritage Characteristics

Chapter 6

The Change That Comes with Courage

Glen

AT THE HIGH SCHOOL where I taught for twenty-eight years, the students would pass down words of advice to other students via handwritten "tip books." Year in and year out, one of the pieces of tried-and-true advice was, "Ask Mr. Schuknecht about the courage it takes to turn down an éclair, and you won't talk about math for an entire class period." It was uncanny. Every year, there were different students and different tip books but the same piece of advice. I guess the kids really didn't want to talk about algebra.

The éclair story was true—if the students asked me about the éclair, they certainly would avoid homework that night because as much as I loved teaching math, I loved teaching my students about courage more. I truly believe teaching about courage is one of the keys to producing strong, successful, and godly students. And, for me, it all starts with the courage to step away from an éclair.

I would start the story by describing a perfect, chocolaty éclair sitting in a bakery window. The filling, creamy and white, oozes out the ends, and the chocolate icing shines in the sun. It looks amazing. I would tell the students to imagine that they are standing on the sidewalk looking through the bakery window, craving that perfect, beautiful, creamy éclair.

But then I would break into their drool-worthy reverie to remind them that it's the middle of their basketball season, or that they have an upcoming gymnastics competition or a band concert—some major event—and the coach or teacher has asked them to lay off the sugar. They are required to eat healthy and stay hydrated. Now, I promise I was not trying to get a bunch of kids to start dieting. I'd just found that nothing speaks to a bunch of teenagers like pastries.

They shouldn't eat the éclair, no matter how badly they want it. The students always groan and moan at this point, but I keep talking. Obviously, the best solution is just to walk away—to turn away from the éclair and go home and have a salad, I tell them.

And then I would pause and make a suggestion. What if they step inside the bakery for a second just to get a whiff of the éclair. They won't eat one, or even buy one; they'll just smell the delicious scent in the bakery. It's not like it's unhealthy to smell an éclair, is it?

And I would tell them to imagine going into the bakery. I tell them to sniff the sweet air, to look at all of the delicious pastries in the case at the front, to look at the plate of éclairs in the window. Even imagining avoiding that éclair gets a little bit trickier now, so I keep pushing. The groaning continues.

Then I would suggest that maybe they should just buy the éclair, not to eat it, of course, but bring it home so they can smell that sweet scent any time they want.

Of course, things always quickly slide downhill from here. The éclair ends up in the refrigerator on a plate, and they wake up at one in the morning—nothing good happens after midnight but sleep—with a rumbling stomach and no willpower. Then before they know it, they would've devoured the éclair alongside a large glass of milk—and eaten a bag of chips to boot.

And then I would write the moral of the story on the board: have enough courage to make sure the éclair never gets close to your refrigerator. Yes, that's right. It takes courage to leave the éclair at the bakery. There are éclairs everywhere in this world, things that look good and smell good and may even have a reputation for being good, but aren't, in fact, good for us.

And it's the kids (and adults) who have the courage to walk away from the éclair who live connected, God-centered lives.

Peter's Courage

Peter was a wild one.

Everyone knew Peter was wild—the teachers, the students, and especially the overprotective fathers of beautiful thirteen-year-old daughters. So I was surprised when he walked into my classroom one day during our weekly On-Track Bible study. The weekly Bible study had grown quite a bit, and many of the football players and track stars were now coming. They were studying the Bible, growing in their faith, joining together in a courageous promise not to fall into the traps of drugs, alcohol, and promiscuity. They were great kids—strong in their faith and coming from Christian families—men and women who could one day lead churches, lead strong Christian families, and be heritage builders themselves.

Peter was a star athlete from a prominent family in town, but he was nothing like the others. He had built himself quite a reputation. Peter's two elder brothers had been showing him the ropes from an early age. He had started distributing pornography to his friends while still in elementary school and began drinking and smoking in the sixth grade. While he hadn't dabbled in sex in middle school, he had big plans to change that in high school.

I had written Peter off as a troublemaker from the first week of school, assuming he was too far down a bad path to be saved. I had warned my own daughter, Alisa, to stay far, far away from him. And I certainly never expected him to walk into my classroom, sit in the back row, and pull out his sandwich as if he wanted to participate in the Bible study.

Peter later confessed that when someone had invited him to the Bible study, his first thought had been that he wanted nothing to do with the boring, religious kids. But then he had decided to show everyone that he too could be religious if he wanted to. He wanted to check attending the Bible study off of his list. But he was astonished that day during lunch. He saw young people so passionate about God that they were willing to risk being made fun of. He saw prayer and compassion and kindness. He saw hope.

And the very next week he returned to the Bible study with a different plan. He no longer wanted to make fun of the guys who attended. This time, he wanted to figure out what he was missing out on. He had always assumed that being a Christian was boring. But in the presence of people who were worshipping, he had become convinced that he was the boring one.

God changed Peter in one week. Curled up on the floor and crying, he gave his life to the Lord that second time he visited my classroom. And he was never the same again.

God took a kid I had long ago given up on and changed him in an instant. He gave him a passion for the things of Christ. That year as Peter grew, I watched his fire for the Lord ignite. I watched an evangelical spirit emerge. I watched him become a man that I was proud to know, proud to mentor. Peter became a leader and often taught during our Wednesday lunch meetings. And though they were good, Peter's words were nothing compared to his passion and courage. Kids wanted a piece of that.

Peter is now a pastor of a small church in San Marcos, Texas. And what's more, Peter is married to my precious daughter, Alisa, and is the father of four of my grandchildren. The kid I had warned my daughter to stay away from has become the man to whom I have entrusted some of my most precious gifts, the man who treats my daughter with such kindness, respect, and love that I have never worried for her.

What's more, he is a spiritual leader to his family, a heritage builder who has the faith to stand tall and the courage to raise kids who, I pray, will also have steadfast faith. My wife and I sit under Peter's teaching every Sunday now, and he is a gifted pastor.

What changed Peter? I think we would all agree that it was God—the

God who has the power to do anything and everything that we could ever imagine and to change the hearts of those who seem lost beyond redemption. To Him be the glory!

But Peter had a part in the transformation too. God gave Peter the courage to say yes, to change his mind, and to open his eyes, and he did it. It took little courage to walk into that first Bible study meeting intending to make fun of the kids in the room. But it took a boatload of courage—courage that would have probably stopped many people—to walk into that second meeting, to admit that maybe there was something to this God thing, and to confess that he was wrong. It took real courage to take the verbal abuse hurled from people who liked the old Peter. And most of all, it took courage to return the éclair to the bakery and change.

How many of us have that kind of courage? And what's more, how many of us Christian parents are raising kids to be courageous enough to walk back in, to change their minds, to listen to that niggling as it tells us to listen up, to hear what Christ has to say?

Courage is a tough attribute to instill in our kids. I've been an educator for over forty years, and only a handful of my students have possessed this kind of courage. Courage is rare in kids of any generation, but it is especially rare today, so when they do have real courage and can stand tall when faced with persecution, they can change the world. These are the kids whom I remember. And these are the ones whom God uses.

Definition of Courage

I define *courage* as doing what you don't want to do, as best as you possibly can. Basically, courage is walking away from the éclair with a smile on your face and a spring in your step.

- It's choosing to study when it would be more fun to go to the football game, watch TV, play video games, or get on social media.
- It's reading the Bible every morning, even when you are so exhausted that you would rather sleep.

- It's choosing to be real and transparent about your struggles, instead of stuffing them inside.
- It's choosing to be honest no matter what, with both words and actions.
- It's choosing to do your work and not plagiarize or cheat, knowing that who you are in the process is far more important than what you are striving for.
- It's focusing on integrity—on saying and doing what's right even when no one would know that you did something wrong.
- It's faithfully attending youth group when you'd rather stay home and watch *The Amazing Race*.
- It's putting in the time and practice it takes to be a great athlete, musician, actress, or artist, even when you feel tired or worn out, or it is too hot outside.
- It's choosing to be kind to people who aren't like you, who you don't agree with, or who you don't have anything in common with.
- It's giving your time to the poor, the downtrodden, the widows, the orphans.
- It's giving your money to the church and those who serve in the mission field.
- It's choosing to listen when you want to talk (ouch!).
- It's choosing to speak up when you want to remain silent.
- It's choosing God over yourself.

Courage is hard. There are so many times it would be easier to run straight into that bakery, pay for the baker's dozen, and eat an entire plateful of éclairs. But God doesn't call us to do the easy things. He calls us to do the right things.

And that takes courage.

Courage to Lead

My granddaughter Kate is a natural leader.

Last week, I was in the courtyard at school when I saw Kate's third-grade class run outside for recess. I stood back and observed for a while and saw Kate quickly lead a pack of girls over to the jump ropes to play a game. She's kind and gracious and fun, and she takes charge naturally.

Leadership is a great quality. But what if Kate started leading those kids away from God? What if she took her gang to a quiet corner to gossip instead of to the jump ropes to play? Or what if she started swinging those jump ropes like helicopter blades instead of jumping rope with them? Chaos would erupt. Likely some of the kids would follow, others would walk away, and maybe a few of the other natural leaders would stand up to her. Whichever way it went, she would lose her positive influence. And she would lose friends. And she would dishonor God.

Knowing what is good reflects well on a person. Doing what's good reflects even better. But leading others to do what's right separates the chaff from the wheat.

We had a group of students act like knuckleheads at a camp this summer. I won't go into too many details, but I will say they left their bunkrooms after nightly check-in. One of the kids, whom I consider a top leader, said that he knew immediately that what they were doing was wrong, so he left and headed back to his bunk. I was pleased that he knew what was right and followed through on what he knew. But I was disappointed that he did not take the next step and steer his classmates toward good behavior. His leadership could have saved his friends from getting into trouble and me from expending a lot of time and energy sorting it all out.

I love John Maxwell's saying, "He that thinketh he leadeth and hath no one following him only taketh a walk." I like the Shakespearean tone because it makes me feel very smart when I am quoting him, but I also like this quote because it precisely captures the lesson we should teach our kids about knowledge and leadership. Yes, they should know what is right. And, yes, they should do what is right. But many of our kids will also be called to lead—which means that they must make the effort to influence their friends and family members to understand and do what is right as well.

In 1 Corinthians 12, we learn about the diversity in the body of Christ. Each of us has received special gifts that enable us to do great work for God. And those gifts can manifest themselves in many different ways. Among your children, you may have natural teachers, administrators, or discerners of the Word. You may also have natural leaders. A natural leader always seems to gather a crowd, to lead the charge, to make up the game.

Being a natural leader is both a good thing and a bad thing. It is good because God uses great leaders to lead people to His kingdom. If a leader truly craves knowledge of Him, seeks to know Him intimately, and desires to do what is right, many lives will be changed for good. Natural leaders who have a sincere desire to lead well will seek wisdom from those who have gone before. They will crave knowledge. They will do what is right. And they will pull others toward what is right as well.

Being a natural leader can also be bad because not all leaders are great leaders. A leader can have good knowledge but refuse to follow it and thereby lead others in the wrong direction. A leader can also manipulate others for self-serving reasons. If we look at it purely from a leadership-based perspective, Adolf Hitler was an incredible leader. Germany was in trouble in the 1930s. Inflation was so high that workers got paid twice a day. Men and woman typically raced out at lunch to spend every mark they had made that morning because the price of toothpaste and toilet paper would rise by the time they got off work that night.

My mother, who grew up in a German family in Canada, gave my brother and me some 1930s German money. It was printed only on one side. Because of the extreme economic slide, the German government had to flood the market with currency and had no time to let the ink dry so they could print the other side.

Adolf Hitler walked into that dire economy and promised hope, and his promise of a solution won him followers by the millions. People willingly overlooked real atrocities in policy to cling to the proffered hope. And Hitler turned the economy around with incredible speed. The people were spellbound by his charisma and would do anything for him. He led with a power seemingly like none other, but he became possibly the most evil dictator in the history of the world because his leadership wasn't paired with wisdom or a desire to do what is right.

I certainly don't want to compare your kids to Hitler, but gifted leaders bear much responsibility. It takes great courage to lead well. Those who courageously learn to seek God, know Him, bear His image, and desire His will can build up His kingdom. And those who don't can destroy it.

So how do you encourage gifted leaders to become great leaders? You instill courage and give them knowledge. How do you do that? You become a cheerleader—you inspire and encourage them to lead, and you give them the knowledge it takes to lead well—not just book knowledge about science, math, history, and literature, but also the knowledge of God. Knowing that He is sovereign and in control instills courage. Pondering His love for us dispels fear. Understanding His faithfulness motivates us to be resolute and steadfast.

So empower your kids—yes, even the kids who aren't natural leaders—to strive to lead others well.

Help Your Kids Become Courageous

When we think of courage, we think of the movie *Braveheart*. Admit it! The first thing you thought of when you started reading this chapter was William Wallace riding into battle, his flag held high. William Wallace certainly was brave, but you've probably already guessed that watching a war movie with your kids will not teach them courage any more than playing the *Madden NFL* video game will teach them to win the Super Bowl.

Movies aren't real life, although they certainly can inspire. The same goes for video games. I believe firmly that if we want to teach our kids to be courageous, we have to show them what courage means and let them feel it for themselves. This is where the teaching and equipping come in.

When my son was about six, I took him on a father-son bike ride. We rode off on a forest trail and got so caught up in the beauty of the day and the forest that I lost track of where we were. Forty-five minutes later, Troy stopped riding and told me he was exhausted. He asked if I could carry him. It was then that I realized we were miles from home.

But I had the perfect opportunity to teach my son courage, and the bike ride became a lesson. (Okay, I really spent ten minutes trying to figure out how I could send up a flare so my wife would come rescue us.) But after realizing the only way to get home was to ride home, I took a deep breath and prayed that God would give me the courage to do what I had to do. I explained to my son that we had a long bike ride in front of us. That we were both tired and thirsty, and our legs hurt, but that this was an opportunity for us both to show courage, to do something we didn't want to do (ride home) as best we could do it (without crying or whining). Then we set off. And slow mile by slow mile, we made our way home.

Looking back, I think it's a good thing he wasn't old enough to realize his little legs went around on the pedals three times more than mine. The trip required way more courage from him than from me, but we were in it together. We were going to succeed together.

That night, Troy and I went for ice cream to celebrate our courageous victory. Only the conquerors got to enjoy the spoils. And the next day, after I had gotten a good night's sleep and rehydrated myself, I decided that one of my goals as a dad would be to give my kids opportunities to be courageous. I wanted them to try courage out firsthand, see how it felt, and get over the hump of fear so that when the stakes got high—like when they were forced to make courageous decisions regarding sex, drugs, alcohol, pornography, and unethical practices—they would know how to respond courageously.

So I set that goal and started working toward it. I intentionally planned regular activities that I knew would push my kids out of their comfort zones and give them the chance to choose courage. Sometimes my plans failed, but more often, they worked out well. And by the time my kids graduated from high school, they had all had a taste of courage.

And I prayed those experiences would help them walk away from the éclairs they certainly saw in a myriad of windows when they got to college.

Quick Tips for Letting Your Kids Experience Courage

1. Go on a long hike, run, or bike ride together. Push yourselves past what you think you can endure.
2. Make a plan and read the Bible in a year together. Get up half an hour earlier than normal to fit it into your schedules, and hold each other accountable on mornings when one of you would rather stay in bed.
3. Plant a garden together. Spend time every day tending to the weeds and watering your plants.
4. Attend Toastmasters' meetings together, and conquer your fear of public speaking.
5. Sign your kid up for AP or advanced-level classes. Help him or her study every night.
6. Start saving for a big-ticket item like a family vacation or car and then remind each other what you are saving for when you have to skip that weekly Starbucks, eating out, or Friday night movies.
7. Sign up for a class that will teach you a new skill, and practice together. Fly fishing, anyone?
8. Choose a tough, classical novel and read it together. Work through the tough parts and then spend time discussing the meaning.
9. Sponsor an orphan or widow. Make sacrifices to come up with the money when necessary. Pray for your sponsored person daily. And write him or her letters monthly.
10. Volunteer in a local soup kitchen.

C. S. Lewis said that courage (he called it fortitude) is found in all the other virtues, which means that a kid who shows great endurance in the midst of struggle also shows great courage, a child who desires purity also demonstrates courage, and young men and women who strive to lead others well also strive for courage. Because of this, teaching your kids courage is a foundational part of their spiritual heritage. It's the wind beneath their wings—the virtue that helps them soar toward Christ even as they struggle in the face of tribulation.

Chapter 7

The Importance of Responsibility

Glen

I WAS NOT THE kind of guy who showed up for class early.

I was more the kind of guy who startled awake five minutes before class started, threw on whatever clothing items I could find on the floor, and ran across campus to get to class before the professor closed the door.

But on the first day of my senior year, I arrived at my eight o'clock psychology class on time. To my surprise, the room was empty. I had no idea what was going on. I wondered if the professor had canceled the class or if I was in the wrong place. And then I thought my roommate had pulled a prank on me by changing my clock. I clenched my fists. I was going to pummel old Brian when I got back to my dorm room.

But then something wonderful happened: *she* walked into the room. She had long brown hair and big dark eyes. She wore a cute little maroon-colored dress with tiny flowers across the sleeves and a big white collar. The most beautiful girl on campus, she was a cheerleader and the homecoming queen. I had talked to her a few times in the past.

"Good morning," she said, smiling.

"H-h-hello," I stammered. *Good ole Brian and his hilarious pranks*, I thought.

"Can I sit here?" The girl scooted into the desk right next to mine.

My eyes widened in surprise, and I looked down at my clothes. They actually weren't half bad. I looked clean in my new linen shorts and shirt, and I had brushed my teeth. I had even used deodorant and combed my hair. *Way to go, Glen!*

We talked about normal first-day stuff as the room began to fill up.

The girl waved goodbye after class, and I smiled in response. Then she walked away with the stream of traffic.

Now I'm a lot of things, but I'm not dumb, so you'd better believe that I made sure I was first in class again the next day. And, by the way, I wore deodorant and clean clothes again, too. Sure enough, she sat beside me. In past years, making my eight o'clock class on time had been challenging, but that semester, it was a breeze. And on those quiet mornings, we talked about everything from psychology to football to God to life. And that amazing beauty has continued sitting beside me for forty-two years.

The point of this story (obviously) is to always, always, always wear deodorant no matter how late you are, because you never know when you will run into a beautiful woman, and when you do, you don't want to smell like a garbage truck.

In my classroom, I display a John Wooden inspirational poster that says, "When opportunity knocks, it's too late to prepare." This is truth. Opportunity was knocking that morning when the most beautiful woman on campus walked in the door and sat down beside me. I was lucky enough that day to be prepared. It was too late to brush my teeth. But I would like to handwrite this small supplement on that poster: "And when opportunity knocks, Mom won't be there."

My mom wasn't in my dorm that morning, reminding me to groom properly, and neither will you always be on hand to remind your kids to finish their homework, to do neat work, to show up to class on time, to wear deodorant, to tuck in their shirts, to wear matching socks, to brush their teeth. They have to learn to take care of themselves on their own. Your job is to equip them.

You also need to train them to look for opportunities. I was able to visit with a man in the last days of his life, and we got to talking about the John Wooden quote. I asked him if opportunity had ever knocked for him. He thought about it and, to my surprise, told me that it had not. I was sad for him, but as I pondered his answer, I realized that God must have presented many exciting opportunities to him. The man had either not been prepared to respond or not even recognized them. Either way, he lost out.

As a Christian, I know that God blesses me constantly and in many ways. Opportunities abound. Though I have not always been prepared to receive them, I'm sure He has many more gifts all wrapped up and ready to give me. And I wonder how many I have failed to open. The book *The Prayer of Jabez* uses an illustration of a huge warehouse with shelves full of boxes all taped shut. In the boxes are gifts God had planned to give us or is waiting to give us.

We must help our children to prepare for the opportunities God may place before them and to recognize these opportunities when they come.

Remove the Crutch

I completely understand why so many parents fall into the trap of micromanagement. It's because of the way their kids behave. They have kids who show up late to class because they were busy talking next to the lockers, who "forget" to brush their teeth and comb their hair, who procrastinate until the last day and then cram all night, and who leave their math books at school the night before the big test. I understand because I was once that kind of kid and know how many ways I went astray.

When our kids are so terribly bad at figuring out life on their own, we have a tendency to all but take over for them. We remind them to brush their teeth. We set alarms on their watches so they are on time to class. We slip a comb into their backpack so they can comb their hair. We schedule study sessions for projects and sit next to them while they work on every simple step. We become a big crutch that they can lean on anytime they feel like they are going to fall. But as a result, they never feel the need to figure things out on their own.

At the beginning of this chapter I told you I was lucky to have remembered to brush my teeth the day Ellen walked into psychology class. I was actually pretty impressed that I was wearing a clean shirt, and even more impressed that I was on time for class. These may seem like small things, but for me, they were downright miraculous, because I was raised by a giving, kind, caring, smart, and dedicated woman, who happened to be a micromanager.

Don't get me wrong. My mom was wonderful. Every morning she made my brother and me eggs, bacon, sausage, and some sort of grain dish—pancakes or French toast or whatnot. Notice I didn't say "every Christmas morning" or "every Sunday" but every morning. Every single day. It was amazing and delicious. And some days she made my brother and me homemade burgers with hand-cut french fries for our after-school snack. A full dinner came later. I was the luckiest kid on the block. But guess who didn't know how to prepare a bowl of cereal when he got to college?

There was more. Laundry? She folded it neatly and put it in my drawer, color-coded, of course, and stacked in the order that I should wear it. If I had a sports uniform, all I needed to do was strip it off and leave it on the living room floor. It magically reappeared in my drawer, clean and folded, the next day. But guess who thoughtlessly left his towels littering the bathroom floor, much to the chagrin of his bride?

Personal hygiene? She laid out my deodorant and shampoo and toothbrush in the bathroom and double-checked with me to make sure I had used them.

Studying? She sat with me for hours, conscientiously quizzing me with flashcards and mapping out study schedules to make sure I got a little bit done each day and never had a late-night cram session.

Shopping? I didn't need to go shopping. I had people for that.

And while I'd say I was a very kind, considerate, and, yes, grateful young man, I had never really learned the skills I needed to take care of myself, not to mention someone else. I had to learn those in adulthood when the stakes are much higher. And when it caused my beautiful bride much grief.

So while I certainly don't blame you for micromanaging your kids—trust me, there were many, many times I wanted to give my daughter a bit of help as she "cleaned" her room—I'm here to tell you that one of the best ways to prepare your kids for the future and build a healthy, non-codependent relationship in the process is to let them learn to do things on their own. Without reminders. Without help. Without "just giving them a little hand."

At a recent conference, the head administrator at Veritas Academy, Jef Fowler, was sitting on a question-and-answer panel. The first question was, How does your school teach character?

Jef answered as he always does, saying, "Character lessons are best learned through failure, and we give our students many opportunities to fail, and fail dramatically."

The audience laughed, but Jef was serious. Our school is not evil—we don't laugh at kids when they fail—but when our students do fail, we, as their school teachers and parents, are there to help them up again and to help them learn from their mistakes.

As a child, I was not allowed to fail. I had everything handed to me on a silver platter. I lived on easy street—but then I got married and my lovely and loving wife would not take up where my mom had left off.

It was a shock to my system when my wife did not enable me to lack basic skills like my mom had. And the necessary remedial training was something I vowed my kids would never struggle through. My kids have failed. Spectacularly. And I was there to lovingly help them through it, so that they could learn to be better. And, hopefully, they know to wear deodorant just in case opportunity knocks.

Work Together to Come Up with a Plan

Say "come up with a plan" out loud. I'm serious. Practice saying it in front of the mirror. Save it as a sticky note on your computer. Write it on a plaque and hang the plaque on your kitchen wall. Whatever you do, keep this command on the tip of your tongue. Use it often, because these words are one of the keys to getting rid of micromanagement in your relationship.

Let's pretend your thirteen-year-old son keeps sleeping later than he should. (You've long since given up going in repeatedly and waking him up. Right?) As usual, he keeps hitting the snooze button, and you're ready to scream at him to get his behind downstairs. Then he can't find his history book, the only pair of shoes he can find are wet because he left them outside in the rain, and the dog slept on his jacket. As you search under his bed for a dry pair of shoes and frantically put a lint brush to his jacket, you shout to your spouse to throw together a peanut butter and jelly sandwich for him to eat on the way to school. Even with all your intervention, however, you pull into the school parking lot two minutes after the bell rings. And Old Mrs. Yates is getting awfully tired of his tardiness, not to mention his excuses.

What do you do? Scream, yell, rant, and lecture? Maybe try six magic words. When he gets home from school, say, "Hey, you've been late to school a lot lately and mornings are getting really frantic. *Let's come up with a plan.*" Then be silent.

Notice I didn't tell you to say, "I've come up with a plan" or "I'll come up with a plan" but "Let's come up with a plan." He must participate in the planning.

After you say those six words, I want you to wait. Zip your lips shut, sit there, and let him talk it through. Let him reason it out. If he's having trouble finding reason, start asking lots of clarifying questions, like "What will tomorrow morning look like, minute by minute?" and "How do you think that will work?"

Listen 90 percent of the time and talk only 10 percent of the time so that this can be his plan. To be honest, the plan may fail, but that's not important. What's important is that he learns.

If my memory of such planning sessions with my own teenagers serves me well, the first words out of his mouth will be something like, "Well, maybe you could wake me up earlier and actually make sure I'm up."

And to that, you will say, "No, I think you are old enough to get yourself up and ready." Then, if you are lucky enough to have a good story from your own alarm-clock days—say when you missed an important test because your alarm clock turned off in a power outage and you missed the bus—then share it. Connect. Share stories. Avoid the lecture. Grow together.

After a conversation like this, work with him to come up with the plan. Maybe he sets two alarms on his alarm clock each morning. Perhaps he lays out his clothes the night before. Maybe he packs himself a sack breakfast. Or maybe he puts his backpack in the trunk every evening before bed so it's ready in the morning.

One key point here: This has to be his plan. Yes, you may think he should get up ten minutes earlier than he does. Or you may think that he should whip up some bacon and eggs and pancakes each day for breakfast (in which case he can come live with me). But what you think doesn't matter, because it's his plan that he is going to follow to make sure he gets the things done that he needs to get done.

Now, I know you're probably thinking, *We can come up with a plan or strategy, but he's not going to follow it. Yes, maybe for a day or even three days, but not long term. And certainly not on into adulthood.*

And that's where we get to the second part of our own little plan. The part where it's okay when your kid forgets to set his alarm or pack his backpack the night before. That is when you have to let them suffer the consequences. Let them be late for school without an excuse note, miss the bus and have to pay you for a ride or walk or ride their bike to school, go to school with wet shoes, a dirty coat, or no socks.

Let them fail, because that's when things get a whole lot more serious in their minds.

Let Your Kids Fail When the Stakes Are Low

It makes good sense to let our kids make mistakes when they are young and the stakes are low. I think every parent has heard this idea and even agreed with it. But when push comes to shove, many parents have a really hard time practicing it. I see the problem all the time.

A few weeks ago, I stopped by Walmart to buy some school supplies.

Okay, I was buying doughnuts. Same thing. Anyway, while I was there, the mother of one of the kids at our school raced in and bought a poster board, glue, and some stencil letters. She smiled at me and said, "Jimmy's science project is due tomorrow, and he totally procrastinated until the last minute. So we're getting supplies now."

I smiled and kept my mouth shut, because in my sixty-plus years on earth, one of the most important lessons I've learned is that sometimes you speak the loudest by keeping your mouth shut. (See, guys do learn!)

And she looked at me and said something very telling, "I know. I totally should just send him to school without his project done since he was the one who procrastinated. But then he would get a C in science." She paused, then added, "On his report card."

I still smiled. But I thought, *So what if he gets a C on his report card in science when he's in the sixth grade? Yes, if he's a senior and college applications are pending, it matters. But in sixth grade? No one looks at sixth-grade report cards. So why not let him turn the project in late in sixth grade and get that C so that in the future, when it does count, he will know that he can't procrastinate?* But I didn't say that because she already knew it. Just like you do.

The truth is it's hard for us to let our kids fail. And my job isn't to tell you something you already know but to give you some coaching on how to allow your kids to fail in a way that helps them learn valuable lessons while maintaining connection and relationship with you.

So how do you let your kids fail safely? Here are a few tips.

1. Take a Break from the Situation

It's easy to fall into fix-it mode with our kids' problems, so purpose to physically step away from the situation. Equip your kids by letting them do the thinking and solving. If your kid confesses that he has a huge project due the next day and didn't get supplies, tell him you need a few minutes to think and pray, and retreat into your room. If your kid has slept past his alarm three mornings in a row, go make yourself a cup of coffee and consider the implications.

2. Write Down the Behavioral Effects

Make columns with the headings, Now, One Year, and Ten Years, and spend a few minutes writing down the consequences of your kid's failure, through time. For example, in the present, if your child gets a C in science in sixth grade, he or she will have to do extra work, likely need tutoring, and likely lose privileges at home. In one year, he or she may have a few residual issues, maybe a lower-level science class, or have to repeat the grade. But in ten years, there will likely be nothing to record. I doubt your kid will even remember their sixth-grade science grade. They will likely have had just as good a chance of being successful in twelfth-grade science as anyone else.

3. Write Down Character Effects

In sixth grade, a C in science is a pretty big consequence for a kid who failed to turn in a final project after working hard the whole year. I'm guessing it will make him or her think seriously about the issue of procrastination. I'm also guessing it will mean that when the next big project comes along, he or she will be working on it from the get-go. Plus, learning this lesson in sixth grade will likely give incentive to develop a strong work ethic before it really does matter.

4. Have a Conversation

Don't speak angrily or condescendingly or dive into lecture mode. But truly talk with your kid. Relate. Say something like, "Hey, Jimmy. I am disappointed that you didn't start this project earlier, especially since it's already bedtime. We couldn't go get supplies even if we wanted to. But I'm sure you are disappointed, too, because it means your grade is going to suffer and your hard work for the rest of the year won't pay off. What a bummer!" Give lots of hugs and empathy. There is nothing wrong with feeling sad for your child when they fail. Then go on. Say something like, "Since there is nothing we can do about it tonight, short of pulling a crazy all-nighter, I guess we will just go to bed. You can talk to your teacher tomorrow and tell her your plan for finishing the project late, and maybe we can get to it on the weekend."

5. Let Your Kid Solve the Problem

Then let it go. Resist the urge to bring it up again, to lecture, to solve. Instead, hug your kid and act like it never happened. If he wakes up the next morning and asks if you can take him to the store for supplies after school, happily agree and ask him to write up a list. If he writes a letter to his teacher about the issue, help him edit it and find an envelope. Be his helper. Help him make a plan.

6. Hold Firm (and Pray for Strength)

I completely understand that this is the hardest part. We so badly want our kids to do well, to be happy. And it's so easy to fix the problems. But hold firm. Stand strong. Be kind and compassionate—but strong. Be an equipper, not an enabler.

I want to end this section with a little pep talk. I know this is hard. I remember having similar issues with my own kids and wanting with my entire being to fix things for them. I wanted to go buy the supplies, to research the paper, to fold the laundry that they had stuffed under their bed. At the heart of being a parent is wanting to make things great for our kids.

But more importantly, we want to inspire our kids to be great. Great kids are confident in their own skills and abilities. They see themselves as capable and able to solve their own problems, which comes by way of experience. Step back and let them learn to see themselves not as kids who need you in order to be successful but as kids who can stand on their own two feet.

Let me reassure you: By enabling, you are hindering. By fixing, you are impairing. You will build a much stronger, much healthier relationship with your kids if you allow them to learn, grow, and thrive on their own.

For the record, it's great to make a breakfast of eggs, bacon, sausage, and waffles for your kids. They will greatly appreciate it. But then, in exchange, have them get up early on Saturday morning and help you make a special meal for the family so that they have important life skills that only come with practice.

I know your kids will appreciate having good cooking skills because I

endured a lot of teasing when as a freshman in college I admitted that I
didn't know how to make a peanut butter and jelly sandwich.

Quick Tips for Creating Fair Expectations

When Ellen and I speak at parenting events and conferences, a lot of parents ask us for fair expectations of responsibility. They want to know if a
third grader is emotionally mature enough to keep track of a project dead-
line, or if a twelfth grader is old enough to cook his own dinner. While each
decision depends on the particular child, here are a few guidelines for what
you can expect your kids, in various age groups, to do, and what you can
give them a little help with.

Age	Fair Expectations	How to Help Without Micromanaging
Pre-K–Kindergarten	Put dirty laundry in the hamper or basket Help put clean laundry in drawers Pick out clothes to wear Lay out clothes or uniform at night Get dressed Check that the backpack is loaded with the right books and is in the right place Put lunch and water bottle in the backpack Help set or clear the table Help cook Follow a bedtime routine Follow a morning routine	Make a step-by-step instruction chart, e.g., on the bedtime routine row attach pictures of putting on pajamas, brushing teeth, and reading a book Provide reminders, e.g., attach a laminated 3x5 card, listing needed items, to the backpack Permit encounters with consequences, e.g., if socks can't be found, let them go without; if a clean shirt can't be found, let them wear a dirty one
1st–3rd Grade	All previous tasks Feed, clean, walk, and bathe the family pets (depending on the pet)	Provide cover for pets' needs; don't let a pet suffer but charge 25 cents for filling the water dish

Age	Fair Expectations	How to Help Without Micromanaging
1st–3rd Grade (con't)	Present uniforms or sportswear for washing, then fold and put it all away Pack lunch and fill water bottle Tell parents about all homework, field trips, class events, projects, and assignments Help keep track of due dates Make the bed Keep room tidy Help with dishes Fasten shoe laces and buckles Order own meal at restaurants Write grocery requests on the list and find the items at the store	Provide a calendar for tracking dates. Have your child place a star on a due date or special event date, then put Xs in squares daily Teach list-making for achieving goals, e.g., help to write a list of needed supplies and the steps it will take to complete school assignments Help them devise a system of organization for where to put their clothing
4th–6th Grade	All tasks from Pre-K–3rd grade Keep track of due dates and weekly schedule Get up on time in the morning Plan in advance for the inclusion of athletic events and parties House chores, e.g., empty the dishwasher, sweep, mop, dust Make simple healthy meals, e.g., sandwiches, cereal, or scrambled eggs	Provide a daily planner and assist in maintaining it accurately Stock the house with easily made snacks Have family sit-down meals and require help with cooking and cleaning Keep a chore list and allow extra chores for extra allowance
Middle School	Mastery of the 4th–6th grade skills Plan household projects, e.g., organize closets or build a bird house. Investigate materials, costs, timeline, etc. Launder own clothes and towels Wash, wax, and detail the car Remember classroom instructions for homework Understand basics of cooking meals and cleaning the kitchen	Supervise a meaningful project, e.g., planting a garden or making a rock path Create kits, e.g., a car cleaning kit with leather wipes and tire cleaner, or a meal planning kit with a budget calculator and a cookbook

Age	Fair Expectations	How to Help Without Micromanaging
High School	Mastery of all the above Wash and change bed sheets each week Maintain a vehicle (if driving), e.g., pay for oil changes, buy gas, and keep the car clean Budget for auto insurance, cell phone, clothes, and extras (e.g., prom dresses, movies tickets) Advocate for themselves with teachers, coaches, and other parents Apply for jobs, internships, and colleges	Supervise first attempts, e.g., first oil change appointment or tire change Give an allowance for food, clothes, and school supplies, and freedom in spending it
College	All normal adult responsibilities Talk to professors about grades and difficulties File for financial aid File for admission, registration, and classes Find a place to live Create and keep a budget	Be available to answer questions via phone calls and emails Be willing to explain paperwork and answer questions Encourage; cheer them on

We Texas Longhorn fans spent a good portion of the early 2000s cheering on fan favorite Colt McCoy as he led the Horns to victory after victory. We loved him, of course, because he helped our precious Horns win but also because he is a young man of integrity who had worked hard to achieve his success. A few years ago, I read the book *Growing Up Colt* written by Colt and his father. In one part, Colt's dad admonishes parents to "prepare your kids for the path, not the path for your kids." That clever saying really struck me. No wonder Colt was such a strong, successful man. He had been prepared for the path—whether it wound uphill or down, through ravines or over mountains. He was prepared. I want my own grandkids (and your kids and grandkids as well) to have that same preparation so that they can face whatever the path throws at them. It starts with responsibility.

And ends with kids who are strong, resilient, courageous, and ready.

Chapter 8

The Raising of Peacemakers

Ellen

MY DAD HAD A temper.

His temper didn't spring up very often, but when it did, I felt utterly, helplessly terrified. I still remember the hard look he'd get in his eyes, the rapid march toward me, and the brutal slap across the face. I preferred the times when he grabbed me by the hair and shook me.

My dad had many redeeming qualities, and I remember him fondly, but he had an anger issue that, at times, made him abusive. For me, as a child, his anger was terrifying. And it was confusing. And I couldn't quite figure out how to avoid it. But now, looking back, I believe his anger was the only way he knew to handle conflict.

When my dad felt extremely angry or disappointed, his habitual means of coping was exploding. Exploding didn't relieve his anger, but it did distance him from the rest of us. And I didn't understand how to build a bridge back to him. Instead, I backed away and avoided him when I sensed his frustration growing.

When I was in middle school, I began biking down to the neighborhood church youth group. I remember hearing a sermon about Matthew 5:9— blessed are the peacemakers—and deciding that, unlike my father, I was going to be a peacemaker. I was going to refuse to take offense, refuse to get angry, and refuse to treat my own family the way my father treated me. Only after many years of confusion did I realize that there is a difference between peacemaking and avoiding conflict.

For a long time, Glen and I were stuck in a conflict pattern that weakened our marriage. Our struggle went something like this: Glen would say something or do something (small) that would upset or offend me. I would feel hurt and upset. I would remind myself that I shouldn't take offense and that I had to be a peacemaker, and I wouldn't say anything. I would grit my teeth, remembering the way my father had treated me, but I would keep my feelings to myself. The incident would continue to bug me, but I would keep pushing the thoughts away, out of my mind.

That issue would niggle at my soul, and after a week or two, Glen would do something else (small, again), and the dam would burst. I would cry, scream, and say things I didn't mean, and we would have a huge argument. Ironically, my efforts toward peacemaking always resulted in me exploding.

Through this type of conflict resolution, I was quickly becoming the person I had vowed not to become. And Glen and I did not grow closer together. Instead, anger, bitterness, and resentment seeped into our marriage, and our relationship fractured.

I prayed about this—a lot. And I realized that I was not the peacemaker I wanted to be. I knew I had to change to save my marriage, and also to give my kids a better future. I had to break the cycle of abuse that had started with my father's father (and probably further back). I couldn't let my kids grow up with the fear and terror that I had grown up with. And I couldn't let the distance that had separated my father from me also separate my kids from me. I had to learn to be a peacemaker.

After an angry outburst, my dad would simply act as if nothing had ever happened. Though I felt hurt and ashamed and angry, he would act aloof and uncaring. I do believe he regretted the anger, but he just did not know how to work through it. We never had resolution. And even though my dad became a believer in his seventies and grew more gentle in nature in his later years, I always felt a bit uncomfortable around him. After his death, I mourned the fact that we had never truly connected as father and daughter.

Dealing with conflict honestly and openly is essential to maintaining healthy relationships. In fact, the depth of love hinges on the quality of honest communication between two individuals. Proverbs 27:6 says that the wounds of a friend are faithful. Furthermore, Ephesians 4:25 exhorts us to put away falsehood and speak the truth with each other, because we belong together.

I believe we have a responsibility to honor God and speak out, especially in our closest relationships. Peacemaking can only be done through honest conversation and willingness to work toward reconciliation. It's hard. It's uncomfortable. But it's right. And if we want to have good, healthy relationships with our kids, our spouses, and our other family members, we have to learn how to recognize problems, confront behavior, and speak truth with each other.

I wanted to believe I was looking out for the other person and seeking peace when I tried to avoid conflict, but really, I was looking out for myself. I didn't want to face the outcome of being honest. I feared being misunderstood and having others grow angry with me, so I chose to avoid dealing with conflict, and just like my dad had done, I allowed distance to creep into my relationships.

I have a sneaking suspicion that you are feeling the weight of conviction right now. I think most of us have a tendency to avoid conflict or explode with conflict (or both), and I think most of us struggle to resolve conflict in a healthy way. Many of us are trapped in relationships in which conflict is never truly resolved and peace is never found. Few of us are peacemakers.

So how do we stop this cycle? How do we become the peacemakers that Matthew 5:9 calls us to be?

To start with, we need to take the time to prayerfully evaluate the emotions surrounding the situation. Galatians 5:22–23 describes the fruit of the Spirit as love, joy, peace, patience, kindness, goodness, faithfulness, gentleness, and *self-control*, so turn to prayer to get a handle on what you are actually feeling. Allow the Holy Spirit to restore your heart to calmness despite feelings of anger or sadness or despair—to help you regain control of yourself. Proverbs 19:11 says that "good sense makes one slow to anger, and it is his glory to overlook an offense." This doesn't mean just ignore offenses or not talk about them, but instead, allow the anger over offenses to subside so you can have uplifting, honest conversations without letting anger seep in.

Next, once you have prayerfully considered your emotions, it's time to actually be a peacemaker. Conflict with others is a necessary part of relationships—it's unavoidable, and it builds connection. Yes, that's right, we actually grow closer when we resolve conflict. Conflict is not the enemy! The enemy is distance. So once you have evaluated your own emotions, choose to bridge the gap and extend an opportunity to grow closer. Sit down and have an open, honest, love-fueled conversation. Speak from your heart. Listen carefully and consider the other person's opinions. Be willing to apologize. Be willing to forgive. Be willing to grow.

I am confident that if you pursue a willing, peacemaker's heart, God will move you toward unity and away from discord, toward peace and away from tension. By His strength you will be able to have honest, open communication and grow a closer, more connected relationship.

It starts with you. And a willingness to really be a peacemaker.

Jesus, the Ultimate Peacemaker

I wonder what it was like to live in a home as a sibling of Jesus. According to most scholars, James was Jesus's sibling, which adds a personal perspective to his book and certainly to his description of "wisdom from above" (James 3:17). He knew firsthand how Jesus carried out his life as the ultimate peacemaker. He knew Jesus to be "pure, then peaceable, gentle, open to reason, full of mercy and good fruits, impartial and sincere." Following our Savior's example would certainly cultivate peace in our families, so ask yourself these questions:

- Pure. Are my motives pure when I address conflict with others, or am I trying to get my way or manipulate others into doing what I want them to do?

- Peaceable. Do I approach others with a peaceful mind-set?
- Gentle. Am I gentle, or do I tend to grow harsh when confronting shortcomings in family members?
- Open to reason. Do I listen to and thoughtfully consider the viewpoints of others? Am I "quick to hear, slow to speak, slow to anger" (James 1:19)?
- Full of mercy and good fruits. Am I quick to condemn and criticize, or do I really forgive and extend grace?
- Impartial and sincere. Am I honest and lovingly direct with others, or do I grumble behind their backs?

James has given us what I consider an ideal framework of a peacemaker, which I take to heart. While I surely make mistakes, I hope that when I deal with conflict now, I am able to act in a way that is pure, peaceable, gentle, open to reason, full of mercy, and sincere.

James concludes this portion of his book with a reminder that peace sows peace: "A harvest of righteousness is sown in peace by those who make peace" (James 3:18). We have to apply this principle to every conflict that takes place in our families if we want to have strong, connected relationships with our kids—and if we want our kids, in turn, to have strong, connected relationships with others.

In the following section, I will discuss both sibling conflict and spousal conflict and give you ideas for helping your kids follow Jesus—the ultimate peacemaker—as you resolve conflicts in your family and strive to build strong relationships.

Sibling Conflict

There is still a giant, bickering, whining elephant in the room: sibling conflict.

You have probably read this chapter about peacemaking and agree wholeheartedly. You want to be a peacemaker. You want to build relationships. You understand your bent for fight-or-flight conflict. And you want to do better.

But what about your kids? How do you convince a stubborn, emotional preteen to be a peacemaker when she is ranting about the fact that her sister stole her favorite shirt? Or worse, how do you kindly and empathetically help a toddler having a tantrum up off the floor after his brother wouldn't share his favorite toy truck?

The short answer: You don't. And you do. Teaching our kids conflict resolution is a long-range project. It's not an in-the-moment, say-you're-sorry-and-make-up thing. It's more of a conversation—a long, long conversation where there will be lots of bumps, bruises, and shouts of "He isn't sharing!" along the way.

RITE is a great framework for this process. In the middle of the commotion—yes, at that moment when someone is crying, someone is screaming, and someone is throwing Play-Doh—you stop the conflict. You sit down with your kids, and you help them to come to an agreement (relate). Then you help them see why resolution is so important, showing them what their relationship could be instead (inspire). You show them how to apologize and actually mean it, and you demonstrate what compromise is (teach).

After the conflict is resolved—through the first two phases of RITE— have ongoing, long-standing conversations that prepare your kids for future conflict resolution. Sometimes you have to give them the actual words. Teach them to make statements using this model: "When you _____, you made me feel _____." For example, "When you left without telling me, you made me feel like you were upset with me." Or, "When you didn't let me play, you made me feel like I am not good enough to be included." And train your kids to express what they are feeling honestly, yet kindly, by saying something like this:

- Hey, when you took my shirt yesterday, I felt really upset because you didn't ask. It felt like you didn't respect me enough to ask me if you could use my things. Can we talk about how we can avoid this type of conflict in the future?

- I really love your blue truck. I know it is yours, but do you think I could play with it sometimes, too?
- When you screamed at me and slammed your door, I felt like you didn't like me or want to be around me. Is that true?
- I got really angry last night and said some things I didn't mean. I exploded! I know that's the wrong way to respond, and I'm sorry. Can I try again to tell you how I felt, without blowing up?

Once your kids have the idea of what to say, encourage them to practice it when they face conflict. Model what conflict resolution looks like. Show them that it's not scary to have tough conversations and that conversations build relationship. Starting when your kids are young, help them learn to value connection and to understand that connection isn't built on always getting along, but rather on finding ways to make peace in the midst of conflict.

I feel the need to say one last thing here: it's super important not to become your child's peacemaker. If you manage their conflicts for them—"say you're sorry" or "stop being mean and start sharing"—you aren't doing them a service. You are allowing them to use you as a crutch. Instead, teach them how to resolve conflict themselves and then let them practice.

Husband and Wife Conflict

Glen and I very, very occasionally have conflict.

Okay, so that was a joke, in case you didn't read the sarcasm between the lines. Because Glen and I are wired very differently, we have struggled with conflict for years. We still do! But, for the sake of our kids (and our grandkids), we have worked hard to learn how to live peacefully with each other.

For years, I thought he needed to see things as I did and learn to respond as I did. I assumed that if he were just like me, we could live peacefully with each other. How shortsighted of me! God did not design Glen to be like me. He designed Glen to be Glen. I had to drop my aim of changing him, and adjust my focus onto my own heart in order for peace to have a chance.

Slowly I began to realize that applying these peacemaking skills in my marriage was a powerful way—perhaps the most powerful way—to train our kids to be peacemakers themselves. I am amazed at how much our kids are still affected by how Glen and I treat each other.

Quick Tips for Forming Peaceful Practices

1. Focus on the real enemy. Satan himself is behind dissension and strife. While we certainly cannot blame our bad choices and actions on the Devil, we would be wise to recognize his strategies to cause division, to break up families, to grow irreparable hurt between loved ones. My husband is not my enemy, although at times I have treated him as if he were. "For we do not wrestle against flesh and blood, but against the rulers, against the authorities, against the cosmic powers over this present darkness, against the spiritual forces of evil in the heavenly places" (Eph. 6:12).

2. Pray. Before engaging in any difficult conversation, pray. Fight your battles with spiritual armor. Ask God to give you His perspective and seek His counsel about what to say and do.

3. Be thoughtful about the timing. When my husband is upset or tired, it's best to put off any difficult conversation until later. While I prefer to get difficult conversations out of the way quickly, he needs to work himself into a right frame of mind to talk about a touchy subject. Rushing the process merely deepens the rift. With kids it might be different. Early responses are often wise with kids, in order to prevent small issues from growing large. At the same time, it's important to wait for teachable moments, when they are not angry or unrepentant. Just like us adults, they need time and space to sort through their feelings before their hearts will soften enough to receive instruction.

4. Listen. Then listen some more. Once you begin the conversations, give ample time to the process of reconciliation. Try to discern the

other person's thoughts and feelings. Ask for clarification. Refrain from judging and accusing. Be patient.

5. Sandwich your discussion. Although you have a point to make and feel rather urgent about making it, begin and end each conversation with affirmation—honest affirmation. Kids and adults alike sense hypocrisy quickly. Find a way to give positive, meaningful, and true affirmation to your spouse to show that, regardless of the current conflict, you love and respect him or her.

As I said above, peacemaking is one of the most essential characteristics of a connected family. A great way to encourage peace is to memorize Scripture verses that stress the importance of becoming peacemakers, together. To start you off, here are some of my favorite verses about this topic:

- Matthew 5:9: "Blessed are the peacemakers, for they shall be called sons of God."
- Romans 12:18: "If possible, so far as it depends on you, live peaceably with all."
- Ephesians 4:2–3: "With all humility and gentleness, with patience, bearing with one another in love, eager to maintain the unity of the Spirit in the bond of peace."
- Colossians 3:15: "And let the peace of Christ rule in your hearts, to which indeed you were called in one body. And be thankful."
- James 3:17–18: "But the wisdom from above is first pure, then peaceable, gentle, open to reason, full of mercy and good fruits, impartial and sincere. And a harvest of righteousness is sown in peace by those who make peace."
- Matthew 5:24: "Leave your gift there before the altar and go. First be reconciled to your brother, and then come and offer your gift."
- Isaiah 26:3: "You keep him in perfect peace whose mind is stayed on you, because he trusts in you."

- Hebrews 12:14: "Strive for peace with everyone, and for the holiness without which no one will see the Lord."

Conflict with others is merely a normal part of living with others. It does, however, have a significant effect on our relationships. Through conflict, either we grow stronger together or we grow distant. Either we work through our differences and bridge the gaps that separate us or we separate ourselves. Teaching our kids and being examples of how to manage conflict wisely gives them the ability to form strong, accountable, and loving relationships that will last, giving you the chance to impart a spiritual heritage and them the opportunity to carry that heritage on for generations.

Chapter 9

The Power of Prayer

Ellen

I'VE TALKED A LOT in this book about my childhood.

In many ways, my childhood was rough. My parents were honest and hardworking, but they were often too busy to pay any attention to me and my siblings. Additionally, neither of them became a Christian until later in life, so we didn't go to church as a family on Sundays or pray around the table. We didn't talk about spiritual things. They didn't teach me about God.

Interestingly, even without a spiritual legacy in my own nuclear family, I grew up enveloped in prayer. Why? Because my grandfather—my mom's dad, Jussi—was a prayer warrior. He understood the power of prayer first-hand and spent his life on his knees, praying for the spiritual health of his kids, grandkids, and later descendants.

His own faith was ignited in the mid-1920s; Jussi had left his home in Kalajoki, Finland, to go to Canada to work on the railroad. In war-torn Finland there was very little work, and he desperately needed to provide for his growing family. So he headed overseas in hope of earning enough money to support his wife and two kids during the upcoming winter. Unfortunately, several Russians had the same idea. Jussi found himself working side by side with the men who had waged war against his home country just months before. The overall mood of the work camp was tense, to say the least.

One night, he went to take a sauna (as Finns do every week). He remembers walking in the sauna door and laying his stuff down, and the next thing he remembers is waking up gagged and bound on the sauna floor. He realized he had been attacked savagely. He struggled to his feet, covered in bruises and cuts, and found that the sauna door was stuck tight. Then he turned around to see a fire blazing in the wood-burning stove. He rattled the door, to no avail, realizing quickly that whoever had beaten him had intended to kill him. He was stuck. As the room grew hotter and hotter, the pain from the cuts and bruises he had received increased, making it difficult to breathe. Knowing that death was near, Jussi thought of his family back home. He pictured his young wife, Saimi, and his small son and daughter. He longed to be in the comfort of their presence.

Jussi remembers his emotions moving from despair to anger to desperation to peace—a peace that transcended understanding. He felt as if he had been overcome with the spirit of someone or something much bigger than himself. For the first time in his life, he felt the actual presence of God—a God he had never paid much attention to before but one who was filling him to the core of his being at that very moment of need.

"*Rakas Herra,*" he cried. "Dear God. Save me!"

In that moment, he remembers three mysterious men opening the door and lifting him out of the blazing hot sauna. They set him down gently in the snow and calmly walked away. He blinked several times, then made his way into the boardinghouse where he was staying.

That miraculous rescue was a turning point in Jussi's life. He left that sauna physically and emotionally broken from the beating and the near-death experience, but his soul had come alive for the first time. His body and mental health were so broken that he had to leave his job at the railroad. Although he returned to Finland and spent years in a troubled, emotional state, he considered his time in Canada a time of redemption. And he never wavered in his conviction that, in response to his prayer, angels had come to save him. As the years passed, Jussi's faith deepened and his dedication to the God who had saved him grew more steadfast. To his dying day, he remained a man steadfast in prayer.

I remember walking, as a young girl, through the fields on the family farm in western Oregon and thinking of my grandfather praying for me back in Finland. It made a difference. I felt stronger somehow. Carried. And I felt connected to something larger than myself. Knowing that my grandfather had survived a horrific ordeal by prayer strengthened and encouraged me. Then when I came to a youthful faith, through Sunday school, I felt a deep connection with my grandfather who lived so far away.

I sensed that somehow, and against the odds, God would save me just as He had saved my grandfather. So I too began to depend on prayer and to press into God. I began to trust in the power of the one thing we can do when everything else fails: pray to the One who controls every little thing on earth.

Give Your Kids a Legacy of Prayer

Prayer is interesting. On a macro level, it's hard even to contemplate that we can talk to the Creator of the universe, the omnipotent, omnipresent One. I mean, by simply turning to Him, we have a direct line of communication with God. That is amazing. And on the micro level, prayer has all kinds of nuances. For me, the idea that we can change the course of our lives through prayer is hard to wrap my mind around. I can hardly believe that my words and cries reach the One who controls everything. Likewise, it's hard to understand how I am to pray believing God will answer my prayers, all the while knowing that He won't give me all that I ask for. Nevertheless, according to Philippians 4:6, I am not to be anxious about anything but in everything by prayer and supplication with thanksgiving let my requests be made known to God.

I don't understand prayer. I struggle to wrap my mind around its power. But I do know that God has called us to pray unceasingly. He has called us to pray in every situation and to make our requests known with thanksgiving.

And He has called us to pray because we trust Him. So that's what I strive to do.

I began to keep a prayer journal in 2001, and at the time of this writing, I have filled forty-five books. In them, I have recorded my daily prayers and meditations, as well as, at times, God's answers. I am utterly certain that much of my growth as a Christian and the direction I have taken in life are attributable to keeping a prayer journal through the years.

If my family were to read my writings, they would not like everything they would see because I have chosen to be honest and lay before the Lord my true thoughts and feelings. Thankfully, God has molded my thoughts in the process. I've written to the Lord with a hurting heart about the times I have felt misunderstood by my husband or someone else. I've prayed for a better perspective from which to respond and that I would be able to see my own fault in matters. I've prayed through the times I have felt anxious over a matter concerning a family member. I could fret and cling to my fears, as if I had some measure of control. But writing to the Lord about everything brings such peace to my soul that I am able to entrust those I love to Him and to cling to Him for my own well-being. I sense that all will be well because He is in control, and I rest, knowing that His presence goes with my loved ones and me wherever we go.

I believe that praying for my family is the most important job I do each day. It rises above every aspect of the RITE approach and should permeate each of its steps. So I make praying a priority—it's the first thing I do when I wake up. I start by giving thankful praise to my Father in heaven. Then, because I believe we first need to know the Lord's will to pray effectively, I ask Him to redirect my thoughts so they align with His. When I begin to see the circumstances through the Lord's eyes, I can pray with greater fervency.

Then I pray for each of my family members—my husband and mom, children and grandchildren. I pray specifically for each of them regarding the areas where they are struggling, the areas where they are excelling, their spiritual growth, and their health. And then I continue on praying for others I have promised to pray for.

Finally, I spend some time recording my prayers and God's answers. Keeping a prayer journal is a strategy that has worked for me, but I don't mean to imply that it is the only way to leave a legacy of prayer. My grandfather's legacy of prayer involved spending hours on his knees every day praying for his family. My husband's involves quiet prayer time at night. In whatever manner you feel best equipped for prayer, that's how you should do it. But my point is that we have to be diligent and faithful in our prayer lives if we want to leave our kids a legacy of prayer.

So pray. Pray every day, intentionally, openly, and honestly. And join in God's work on behalf of your family through the power of prayer.

Get Started

God gave us the great gift of the stewardship of our kids (and grandkids), and one of the greatest stewardship duties is prayer. I consider it a first priority for my family, and I think if you want to build a legacy that is connected, God-loving, and God-honoring, you also will consider it of central importance.

I'm guessing you pray for your kids and grandkids. But a legacy of prayer is more than praying. (You should never put *just* in front of *praying*. That's like saying "just a miracle" or "just our eternal salvation.") Daily prayer for our kids is only the start of becoming the prayer warriors our families need. We have to dig deep into the Scriptures, yearn to know God, and journey toward a healthy, rich, life-changing prayer life with our creator. And then we have to share all that with our kids.

We start by starting. A pastor friend of mine once said something that has stuck with me: we pray as much as we want to. We actually start to lead a prayerful life by wanting to start to lead a prayerful life. When I meditate on who God is, that He asks me to pray, and that somehow my prayer changes things, I begin to want to pray more.

The actual act of praying begins with gratitude. "Enter his gates with thanksgiving, and his courts with praise!" (Ps. 100:4). We acknowledge that "the LORD is good; his steadfast love endures forever, and his faithfulness to all generations" (Ps. 100:5). Thankfulness ushers us into God's presence! There we turn our feelings, our disappointments, our frustrations, our questions, and our concerns into prayers. We let go and give God control. We pause to listen and to contemplate how He directs us. We wait until His peace, which surpasses all understanding, becomes the guardian of our hearts and minds (Phil. 4:7).

Early in our marriage, Glen asked me to pray regularly with him. He would sit down next to me on the couch and wrap his arm around me and pray for our lives, our family, and our dreams. We prayed prayers of thanksgiving and supplication and hope and trust. And I remember feeling a deep sense of security wash over me. I trusted my husband implicitly in those moments. Likewise, when we pray intentionally with our kids—out loud and together—we develop a sense of shared trust and security.

When I had young kids, I could easily fall into the habit of a quick prayer at dinner and bedtime. "Dear Lord, Help So-and-So to sleep well and keep her safe tonight. Amen." Of course, any prayer is prayer, but a prayer like that does nothing to create a legacy of prayer for your kids. Instead, I encourage you to make prayer a conversation between you and God. Set aside time for it—as much time as your kids need—and talk together about what prayer means and how it helps us to connect in a meaningful way with our Creator.

Keep a Record of Answered Prayers

Prayer is powerful. I think we all know that on a factual level, but when life gets busy and things start to go wrong, we can forget about all the times God has answered prayers in great and miraculous ways. We tend to focus on how today's prayers seem unanswered, how today's thoughts seem unguided, and how today's troubles seem multiplied. I am reminded of John 16:33, which says, "In the world you will have tribulation. But take heart; I have overcome the world." If Christ has overcome the world, we must change our focus and take heart.

I often go back and read through those forty-five prayer journals of mine.

My words remind me of the urgency I felt to pray when I had trials and trib-ulations galore and things seemed to be falling apart. When I felt that way, I prayed and prayed and prayed some more. Regardless of disappointment or discouragement, I did not let go of an outcome I had come to believe God wanted. And He answered in big, powerful ways. Here are some examples:

- I prayed and fasted for three days for my son-in-law Cameron, who was fresh out of college and applying for a much-wanted high school coaching job in Austin. He was discouraged, but at the very end of the third day—after closing time in Austin—Cameron received a telephone offer to teach mathematics at the school. While he also received a small coaching assignment, the math position wound up being an even better placement for him.

- My son-in-law Peter received a professional recommendation that he combat lupus with a drug that would leave him infertile. I prayed for days for another solution so that their family wouldn't end up child-less. He took the drug, but even in the midst of terrible illness God miraculously gifted them with four beautiful, wonderful children.

- My daughter Alisa and Peter were still in high school when God gave me a vision that I recorded in my journal. The vision was of them bear-ing much fruit for His kingdom in ministry. It sounds crazy, I know, but I drew a tree with fruit, and underneath it were bunnies, which I felt represented many children. It's one of the reasons that I could not stop thinking of them with many children. My journal drawing also shows a storm cloud over the tree, with a rainbow breaking through. The storm cloud represented many trials that would come against them. I felt the Lord telling me to be faithful to pray for the two of them for years, which I have done since that day. There were times when their relationship fell apart (they broke up for several years in college) and times when reconciliation seemed hopeless (there was a point when Alisa swore she would never speak to him again). But something in me needed to keep praying. One day in Austin, when

I was taking a walk and praying for the two of them, I saw a rainbow, and I remembered the drawing and sensed in my spirit that their hearts were growing together again. Shortly afterward they got engaged. This vision and the resulting years of praying stand out in my mind as one of the most profound prayer journeys God has taken me on. Today as I watch them lead a church together and parent four young children, I remember God's faithfulness and how He blesses us by asking us to join with Him by prayer.

- My son, Troy, and his wife moved to Louisville to go to seminary. While there, they had their first son, Jude, and I struggled with being away from my precious grandson. Okay, I missed my son and his wife too, but, oh, how I missed that grandbaby. So I began to pray for a change. Troy mentioned to me one day that they would be interested in moving back, but they had no idea where to get a job. I simply printed out his résumé and dropped it on the desk of the principal at a local private school. Months later I learned from Troy that he would be flying in for an interview. He got the job and has now been a principal at that school for eight years. And I have been able to spend regular time not just with Jude but also with his three younger siblings.

- When my daughter Alisa sat at my daughter-in-law's baby shower with tears in her eyes, hardly able to participate after having been through years of infertility and a failed adoption, hope seemed elusive. After years of waiting and then finding out that pregnancy was medically impossible, they had believed that their family would include just one daughter. There was nothing else that they could do, except pray. We woke up two days later to the news that a precious little boy—our miraculous, wonderful grandson Asa—had been born, and Alisa and Peter had been chosen for the privilege of adopting him. Two months later, Alisa found out she was pregnant. The power of prayer took them from hopeless to incredibly hopeful in a matter of days.

My list could go on and on and on. In fact, Glen made me delete about twenty thousand words from this list just so this book wouldn't end up being four inches thick. The point is, God answers our prayers constantly. He moves mountains for us. And by sharing God's answers, we are able to show our kids His character and His plans for our lives.

I encourage you to find a place to record answered prayers. If you choose not to keep a prayer journal, you could instead keep a blank book on your bookshelf for family members to jot down God's answers to prayers, or you could keep a list on the fridge. You could even write God's answers on the inside cover of your Bible. One friend of mine keeps visual mementos of answered prayer, such as a pair of socks to represent healing or a picture of a van to represent a miraculous gift. The mementos stay in their kids' bedrooms as visual proof of God's faithfulness and serve as a reminder of the power of prayer. Find a way that will work for you to record God's blessings so that your kids can see exactly how He has changed your lives through answered prayer.

Pray Scripture over Your Kids

My wonderful husband prays a Scripture-based blessing over his grandkids each time he tucks them into bed. He did it for our children when they were younger and will likely do it for our great-grandchildren, if God wills that we have them. I love this tradition so much. God's Word has power, so allow God to lead you to the right Scriptures and pray them over your children out loud and often. Here are a few examples to get you started:

- For the fearful child, pray 2 Timothy 1:7, that the Lord would grant her a spirit not of fear but of power and love and self-control.
- For the prideful child, pray Ephesians 4:17–24, that the Lord would melt away any hardness of his heart.
- For the child that has sinned or made a mistake, pray James 5:16, that your family would confess their sins to one another and pray for one

another, that all may be healed. The prayer of a righteous person has great power as it is working.

- For the child who is anxious or worried, pray Philippians 4:4–7, that she would rejoice in everything and, with prayer and supplication, bring her requests to God and that He would bring peace that surpasses her understanding.
- For the child who is curious and craves answers, pray Jeremiah 33:3, that he would call out to God, and that God will answer him, and tell him great and hidden things that he has not known.
- For the insecure child, pray Lamentations 3:22–24, that she would find the Lord's steadfast love, which never ceases, and His mercies, which are new every morning, and that she may be able to put her hope in Him and say, "The LORD is my portion."
- For the doubting child, pray 1 Thessalonians 2:13, that he would receive God's Word, and accept it not as the word of men but as what it really is, the Word of God.
- For the growing child, pray Luke 2:52, that she may grow in wisdom and in stature, and in favor with God and with man.
- For the child struggling with temptation, pray John 15:7, that she will abide in the Lord and that His Word will abide in her, so that she can ask whatever she wishes, and it will be done for her.
- And for every child, pray Numbers 6:24–26, that the Lord may bless and keep him, make His face to shine upon him and be gracious to him, and lift up His countenance upon him and give him peace.

I am so very grateful for my grandfather, Jussi, who passed forward to me a spiritual heritage of prayer. While my own parents did not come to faith until later in life, God answered Jussi's prayers on behalf of his daughter, my mother, who did eventually become a woman of faith, deeply committed to prayer. Still, at age eighty-nine and struggling with Alzheimer's disease, she prays with fervency. Her communication with people has broken down, but her prayers continue to flow freely. Each time she speaks to her Savior, tears run down her cheeks. Talking is a struggle, but prayer requires her heart more than her mind. Talk about a spiritual heritage!

Instilling prayerfulness in our children begins with us. I don't know how, and I sometimes don't understand why, but I do know that prayer changes things. At the very least, it changes me for the better by turning my eyes to an ever-present, always-available God whose faithfulness extends to all generations.

Quick Tips for Teaching Your Kids About Prayer

1. Make prayer natural. Consider it a conversation between you two and God. So feel free to interject, to talk, to coach your child as you pray together.

2. Spend time praising God. Sometimes with kids, the best way to do this is to sing hymns or other Christian songs, like "Bless the Lord, Oh My Soul" or "Amazing Grace," together.

3. Don't correct or praise. You are having a conversation with God. Your kids should never worry about doing it right or saying something wrong. Let the words flow from your children's hearts to God's ears.

4. Pray in the moment. When your child comes to you with a problem about someone, stop and pray immediately. Don't wait for bedtime or dinnertime or the right time.

5. Keep track of answered prayers. Share with your kids times that you prayed and God answered in unique and surprising ways.

6. Demonstrate an attitude of thankfulness and gratitude. Ask your children about the best parts of their day and then thank God in prayer for those moments.

7. Choose a spot in your home to post prayer requests. Get a white board or a chalkboard or even a prayer journal and encourage all family members not only to share their prayer requests there but also to check the requests of others often and pray for each other.

8. Hold family prayer meetings. My friend Tammy's family has a Wednesday night prayer meeting. Everyone comes and shares prayer requests, and the family prays together.
9. Share your own prayers. Let your kids know specifically how you pray for them on your own.
10. Be affirming in your prayers. It gets tempting to turn your prayer into a lecture: "Dear Lord, help little Sammy learn to be kind, and help Meggy to get her homework done." Resist the urge. Make your prayers positive. Try something like, "Dear Lord, thank you that Sammy was created by you to be a kind, loving child. And thank you that Meggy was given a brain so she can learn and grow."

I pray that these ideas will help you grow a beautiful, enduring, and life-breathing spiritual legacy for your kids, grandkids, and future descendants. Just as my grandfather prayed for me, you can pray for your family. Start praying now and change your family dynamics for years to come, all while sitting in front of the throne of the One who loves you and your children so much that He willingly gave everything for them.

Chapter 10

The Legacy of Faith

Glen

ELLEN OFTEN SAYS THAT she was attracted to me, way back in college, because I had a legacy of faith. (I guess brushing my teeth before psych class wasn't all that important after all.) My parents had raised me under an umbrella of faith and prayer that spanned several previous generations. Ellen says that legacy was a big factor in her wanting to spend her life with me. She says she saw in me, aside from my stunning good looks, a steadfastness and faithfulness that she hadn't seen in others she had dated.

I can't give myself much credit for the legacy of faith that I was blessed with, but she is right. My parents and grandparents set an amazing example of faithfulness in prayer, one that allowed me to embrace my faith at an early age and cling to it when times got tough.

My maternal grandfather, Albert Felberg, was raised in East Prussia. His family farm was right on the border between what is now Germany and Poland. One night when he was about eight years old, his quiet farm was raided by Russian soldiers who were fighting the Prussians in World War I. My grandfather described the chaos of that night as a rapid grab for warm clothes, tearful goodbyes, and his mother screaming that everyone should meet back at the farmhouse as soon as they were able. He was put on a train and wondered if he'd ever see his family again.

The train stopped in Leningrad, and he was immediately shuffled into a prison camp. He and about a hundred other boys were put into a small room. Minutes later, a hazy gas filled the room. My grandfather blacked out, then woke up several hours later on a cold, snow-covered street. He's not sure what happened in that gas chamber. Maybe another child had fallen on him or he had found an air pocket, but somehow, he and two others had survived. The Russian soldiers, under orders to kill all German boys so that they wouldn't grow up to become German soldiers, had thrown the three survivors onto the streets assuming they would freeze to death before they woke up.

He didn't. My grandfather, with burning lungs, stumbled to a nearby garbage can and tried to find something to wrap around his cold, wet limbs. By providence, he found a huge men's fur coat that was so long it dragged on the ground. He spent his first night on the street huddled in the coat. One night turned into two and then ten. He dug through garbage cans to find food. He slept on park benches. And he hid under bridges for protection from storms.

He later told me that he only stole food once during his entire ordeal—and even then he wasn't sure if it would have been considered stealing. He had watched a baker hauling huge baskets of bread from a trailer and asked if he could help in exchange for a loaf (about the size of a hamburger bun) or two. The man agreed and said that if he helped unload the entire trailer, he would get two small loaves—but when my grandfather finished unloading, the man held up his hands and said, "Sorry. Now beat it." My grandfather said he was so hungry that he just grabbed two loaves out of a basket and ran as fast as he could down the street. He felt bad about that for years and says that he never stole again in his entire life.

My grandfather roamed the streets of Leningrad from 1913 to 1917. Then he walked and hitched rides back to Poland and then back to Prussia to keep his promise to meet back at the farmhouse from which he had been snatched. It took months of trekking, but one night he knocked on the farmhouse door and his much-older mother answered. Five of his thirteen brothers and sisters did not survive the war, but eight did, and they made it back home. My grandfather even made it home with his faith intact.

I think many people would become jaded and hard-hearted in this situation. In hopelessness they would become angry. In despair and dejection they would reject God. In hunger and pain they would resort to crime. My grandfather might have succumbed as well, but God used those years on the cold, bitter, war-torn Russian streets to pull him close. God drew my grandfather into a faith so deep and so unmovable that he never once wavered. His faith tested with fire, he came out of the war soft-hearted, resilient, and passionate about God.

My grandfather told me he went on to get a seminary degree and become an associate pastor in a church, where he met Frieda Witt, "the most beautiful woman in Berlin." He took one look at her and knew he had to marry her. But when he asked Frieda out, she wasn't sure her father would approve. Her dad wanted wealth and stature for his daughter, not a poor associate pastor from Prussia. Still, he knocked on the door to a huge, sprawling mansion, and a butler led him to a large sitting room. My grandfather had just sat down when Frieda's father, an enormous man, burst into the room, scowled at him, and shook his hand with an iron grip. He told my grandfather that no poor preacher was to date his daughter and that he should just get lost.

My grandfather later found out that Frieda's father was the Minister of Defense for Berlin. That's like being the police chief, the fire chief, and the army general all rolled up into one. He was one of the most powerful men in Germany, and his family lived with wealth and luxury. Frieda had maids and cooks and chauffeurs and bodyguards. But none of that scared my grandfather.

He went back to that mansion again and again to spend time with her father, to build a relationship, and to share his faith. And you know what? His persistence paid off. A year later, he married my grandmother, Frieda "Jerusalem" Felberg. He continued to pastor his church in Berlin even after Frieda found out she was pregnant. Their daughter, my aunt Ingeborg, was born in 1928. Then, a few years later, when extreme inflation plunged

Germany into an economic depression, Grandma Frieda found out she was pregnant again.

My grandfather knew the evil of war and sensed it was coming again, but he was forewarned this time. His health was still poor from having been gassed and he wanted all his babies to grow up, so he moved the family to Winnipeg, Manitoba, in Canada, where they could enjoy a drier climate and a healthier political atmosphere. That is where my mom, Esther, was born. She was raised in Lodi, California, where he moved the family a few years later.

And the legacy of faith that started in that farmhouse in East Prussia continued. My mom was the quintessential pastor's kid, which (obviously) meant she followed all the rules all the time, no matter what. I'm kidding. She was probably much like many of the pastors' kids you grew up with: fun-loving, Jesus-loving, and friend-loving (and maybe a little mischievous). My mom tells the story that one day she was sitting in church "listening attentively" to the sermon when her father bellowed her name from the pulpit.

"Esther! What's so funny?" he shouted.

Okay, so maybe she wasn't listening that attentively. She and her best friend, Ruthie, had been snickering, and her father didn't cut them any slack. They both spent the rest of that sermon standing up on the stage facing the audience with their hands clasped in front of them.

Things like that never stopped my mom from developing a deep, unwavering love of God and his church. She was strong yet tender, thoughtful, devoted, kind, willing to help, honest, and ethical. And because of that—you guessed it—the legacy of faith that started in a farmhouse in East Prussia continued as she grew into a woman, wife, and mother.

I was born, and my brother wasn't long behind me. We grew up in a home where we were prayed for daily, where we spent time talking about Jesus like He was a best friend, and where we learned to go to church every Sunday, rain or shine. Faith was a centerpiece for our lives, and I lived with an awareness of Jesus being woven into everything we did.

When Ellen and I met, she saw in me something I had yet to notice myself: I carried with me a heritage of connection to God, a legacy of faith, a consistent, generational desire to look to God. And now that I have raised my own three kids and been blessed with eleven grandkids, I look back and know that I haven't been perfect. I have made mistakes. We have faced trials. I have wavered and doubted and struggled. But I have prayed fervently. I have sought Jesus. I have studied His Word. And I pray that the legacy that was forged on the shoulders of my grandfather and my mom has now been passed on to my own children and grandchildren. And that they will pass it along to their children and grandchildren. The legacy grows generation by generation, step by step, prayer by prayer.

You see, a spiritual heritage starts with a parent, you.

Quick Tips for Creating a Legacy of Faith for Your Kids

To be honest, it's a bit lame to write a how-to list for creating a legacy of faith after telling you the stories of two great heroes of the faith. It's obvious from their stories and from thousands of others that creating a legacy of faith takes faith. It takes a brave, courageous, wholehearted love of God and a faith that can move mountains. And no one can write a how-to list for that.

So maybe the title of this section should be something like Ten Quick Tips for Letting Your Legacy Shine, or How to Grow Your Legacy in Ten Easy Steps. But you get the point. I simply can't tell you how to have the rock-solid, never-give-up faith that my grandfather had—that's between you and God. But I can give you some ideas on how faith can shine in your home and in your family so that sixty years from now your kids will look back and say, "Yes. I have it. I have a legacy of faith." Here are some ideas:

1. Write down your prayers. My wife told you earlier in this book that she has written down her daily prayers for almost twenty years now. She keeps stacks of journals in our office, and when she fills one up, she moves on to the next one. This is an amazing legacy for our kids and grandkids because they can see what my wife was praying for at

any given time. We look through her journals and read prayers about our kids' future spouses and kids. Journals from the early 2000s are filled with the big decision of moving to Austin. Since then, there have been prayers about pregnancies, adoptions, grandbabies, and other family milestones. These journals provide beautiful reminders of the power of prayer. They are, themselves, a beautiful symbol of the hours and hours she's spent on her knees praying for our family.

2. Take special note of answered prayers. God so often works behind the scenes over dozens of years to carry out His plans, so taking note of answered prayers goes hand in hand with keeping a prayer journal. When you note the answers to long-prayed prayers—like the birth of a healthy baby, or a healing, or a new job, or a change of heart— you are recording God's consistent faithfulness to your family. One special way to remember God's answers is to collect them on slips of paper in a beautiful box as mementos for your family.

3. Have a daily devotion together. When I was a kid, my dad read from a little white book called *Our Daily Bread* every morning at the break-fast table. I still treasure the memories I have of our family talking about spiritual things over our sausage and eggs. Family devotionals instilled in me a lifelong habit of reading the Bible and spending time with God each morning. I really like *One Year Classic Family Devotions* by Keys for Kids and *Grace for the Moment* by Max Lucado. I also suggest visiting a Christian bookstore with your kids to find a daily devotional that everyone gets excited about.

4. Have a daily quiet time on your own. It's important to set the ex-ample of spending time in God's Word on your own, each day. So whether it's early in the morning before your kids get up or late at night after they have all gone to bed, get in the habit of reading Scrip-ture and praying in solitude every single day.

5. Talk about your spiritual struggles with your kids. Do you occasion-ally doubt God? Or do you struggle to keep your mind focused when you pray? Or does keeping a regular quiet time seem to get away from

you? Tell your kids about it! Let them know that you are struggling with things—probably things that they also struggle with from time to time—and then tell them how you are working through it. Share the ways you're overcoming your problems.

6. Start spiritual traditions. When my kids were growing up, we had a tradition of holding hands and taking time to pray specifically for a person celebrating a birthday. We also had a tradition on Sunday evenings in December during advent of eating Christmas cookies, lighting a candle, singing hymns, and telling successive parts of the Christmas story. My grandkids have a tradition of memorizing the passages of Scripture at the same time, so they can work on it together and hold each other accountable. These traditions are easy, and they have become part of a legacy. You can come up with a few easy spiritual traditions for your family as well, perhaps singing a certain song before bed or memorizing certain passages at certain times, and begin to form your own faith legacy.

7. Eat dinner together whenever possible. We always ate dinner together as a family when I was growing up—if baseball practice ended at eight o'clock, we ate at nine, but we ate together. I carried that tradition on into my own family, and now my kids do it with their families. It's important to have that time as a family to regroup, to talk, to share, and to discuss the day, each and every day. Those family discussions that start by asking how someone's day was often evolve into vibrant discussions about God, politics, relationships, and more that can help build the basis for your kids' growing faith.

8. Tell or read great stories of faith. Stories like my grandfather's powerfully demonstrate what faith looks like. Read to your kids the biblical stories of Paul and Peter and King Josiah. And read about Corrie ten Boom, Booker T. Washington, Frederick Douglass, President Lincoln, and other heroes as well. When your kids have seen what faith looks like, let them start dreaming of their own legacy.

9. Create faith-based milestones. I remember turning eighteen and having to register for the Vietnam draft. Each of my kids remembers the day they turned sixteen and got their driver's license. These are important life events, but they have nothing to do with a developing faith. The Jewish culture—with bar mitzvahs and bat mitzvahs—has this concept right. They celebrate milestones that cement that legacy of faith. They understand the value of a celebrated rite of passage. Your kids could benefit in the same way. Celebrate baby dedications by hanging a photo or a footprint in clay on the wall. Create the tradition of taking an exploratory family heritage trip when a child is nine or ten. Go camping "boys only" with your sons when they turn thirteen, and talk about God. Take your daughter to a cutesy hotel on her fourteenth birthday to talk about womanhood. Forging important memories like these for your kids will lay the groundwork for faith and an understanding that we are each part of something bigger than ourselves.

10. Take time to build legacy at bedtime. When you put your kids down for a nap or to bed, make sure to make that time about legacy. Pray together. Sing favorite hymns from your childhood as you rub their backs. My kids still remember when I did that. Even though I am a terrible singer, they always begged for more songs. Maybe I was a great back rubber! Once I finished, I would always say this blessing over them: "May the Lord bless you and keep you. May He make His face to shine upon you and give you peace. May He teach you courage and show you how much He loves you. Amen."

Quick Tips for Creating a Legacy of Faith for Your Grandkids

As you know, I am now a proud grandfather. While I am unable to routinely help all eleven of my grandkids with things like daily devotions and goodnight prayers, I am fortunate enough to live only a few minutes away, and I can and do nurture them in many other ways. Grandparents can be pretty awesome (if I can say so myself) in the roles they play in their grandchildren's spiritual heritage. So what are some things grandparents can do to help build a spiritual heritage for their grandkids? Here are a few ideas:

1. Create traditions just for you and your grandkids. My wife picks a great novel that she loves—think *Little House on the Prairie* or *The Lion, The Witch and the Wardrobe*—and sets aside a half hour every Tuesday afternoon to read to whichever grandkids want to come hear the story. The kids love it because they get special time with their grandmother, and she loves the time to share her favorite books. Reading a novel together could easily be done long-distance via Skype—just set a standing Skype date every week and read! The main thing is to choose traditions that will help you spend dedicated, meaningful time with your grandkids.

2. Ask to babysit. Babysitting can be hard, especially for old fogies like me. There are nights when the only thing I want to do is watch the Longhorns play, but I volunteer to babysit my sweet (albeit loud and wild) grandkids anyway. Ellen and I both think babysitting is important—not only do our kids get a break from the craziness of parenting young kids, but we get a chance to spend one-on-one time with our grandkids and instill that all-so-important spiritual heritage. If you and your grandkids do not live in the same town, babysitting is even more important—offer to go to stay with your grandkids for a weekend so their parents can have a little getaway, or invite the grandkids to stay with you for a week in the summer. Sure, it will be tiring and stressful, but it will be worth every exhausting moment.

3. Send your grandchild prayers, verses, and thoughts. My daughter Erin's mother-in-law lives several states away from her grandkids, so she sees them only once or twice a year. Still, on a weekly basis she sends letters with pictures of things she's been doing, favorite verses, quick prayers, and little notes. The kids love receiving her letters,

which they save in their rooms. What a spiritual legacy she is giving them, even from a distance.

4. Make a point of spending one-on-one time with each grandchild. Kids need one-on-one attention and time. If you live far away, do it by phone—just call your grandchild and talk to him or her. If you live nearby, you can invite your grandchild to slumber parties or coffee dates or ice cream outings. Whatever you do, make sure you give your grandchild lots of opportunity to talk and share, and also spend some time telling your own thoughts and stories. Allow the relationship to deepen.

5. Find a way to celebrate the big rites of passage. Maybe you will take each of your grandchildren on a trip when they graduate from high school. Or maybe you will invite each grandchild to stay with you for a weekend before they start kindergarten. Maybe it will be a shopping trip, a camping adventure, a long bike ride, or a movie outing. Make an intentional effort to celebrate the big events in your grandchildren's lives in meaningful ways because the result of those efforts will be heart-to-heart connection.

The ideas shared in this chapter are small rituals—tiny things that often would take mere minutes of your day—but they each have big legacy-building results. These little things are what allow your precious kids and grandkids to fall asleep safe in God's arms and wake up knowing they are part of something big and special. And I pray that you too, through careful prayer and intentional conversation, will be able to build a legacy of faith that will sustain your kids, your grandkids, and all your future generations throughout their lives. I pray that through your legacy your descendants will know that God is the ultimate Father, the One who loves us more than we can imagine, and the One who has big plans for you and your family.

Part Three

Extra Tools to Put into Practice

Chapter 11

The Purpose in Each Child's Uniqueness

Ellen

MY YOUNGER TWO CHILDREN, Troy and Alisa, are very similar. Both are focused athletes, the kind of kids who stood in the driveway for hours perfecting their basketball shots. Both are analytical and methodical. They read carefully. They study intensely. They relate carefully. And, what's more, both would be categorized as "emotionally steady"—you know, those people who think before they speak and have an easier time controlling what comes out of their mouths.

Erin, on the other hand is wired more like me—she's creative and passionate and wears her emotions on her sleeve. She's disorganized and impulsive. She's the one who controls the conversations, plans the events, comes up with the ideas, implements, and leads. Her view of any situation is based on how she feels, on the emotions that are coursing through her mind. And, she's quick to speak. Basically, she says what she thinks when she thinks it, and often regrets it later.

As I'm sure you can imagine, our blend of characteristics does not lend itself to quiet family dinners. Our family has conflict because of our differences—quite often. Someone annoys someone else. Someone speaks without thinking. Someone inadvertently hurts feelings. Someone thinks differently than someone else about a certain topic. Contention happens. But I have yet to meet a family that doesn't have these types of conflicts. And if I did meet one, I'm not sure I would want to hang out with them. I firmly believe that we all grow stronger and wiser because of our differences. Things like differences of opinion, personality differences, and yes, even conflicts are good for families.

Over time, I have learned that we need each other and each of us has something to offer that brings balance and strength to a family. If we were all the same, we would have less need of each other. Some people bring introspection and careful thought to a matter. Others bring energy and connection. Some bring leadership. Others, creativity. The optimist brings vision and hope and drive. The pessimist figures out the potential problems by poking holes in the ideas.

Where would we be without our differences? How could we build a loving, connected family that allows each member to shine in the way God created them to shine? By learning how to embrace our differences, to connect through conflict, and to work toward a common goal of reconciliation, we all grow stronger.

Parent the Child God Gave You

As a young mom, I found it easier to parent my introverts.

Troy and Alisa were just steadier. They were less apt to melt down, and they seemed more controllable.

At first I tried to mold my Erin into someone she was not, to make her be like her siblings, one of the "easy" ones. In reality, her personality was similar to mine, and I knew firsthand the trouble we passionate emotion-driven people can get into if we don't learn to think through our words before they fly out of our mouths. Thus, I tried reshaping her into someone else rather than parenting the child God gave me.

This caused—you guessed it—conflict. Erin resisted me passionately. We fought and we argued, and she screamed words that pierced me to my soul. I felt disrespected. She felt misunderstood. I felt hopeless. She felt desperate.

In looking back, I know that I failed to validate who she was by trying to define her differently. Now, I realize that passionate, emotional kids, like Erin, require more understanding, more guidance, and more refining. They often get into trouble simply because of their nature. But that doesn't mean that they are by nature bad or naughty. They are just different. They are each unique and created by our heavenly Father to do great works for Him.

I am not advocating that you take a hands-off approach and let your more difficult kids do whatever they want to do but, instead, that you allow the differences among your children to inspire a deeper connection and understanding within your family. Don't worry; I'll give you some ideas for how to do this later in the chapter.

Passionate, emotional kids like Erin need more affirmation than other children because they need more correction. The inspiring step in RITE is vital because they often wind up feeling so bad about themselves. I remember Erin asking, "Why do I always get into trouble and Troy and Alisa don't?" And I'd respond, "Why do you do the things you do that they don't do?"

One of my regrets as a parent is that, through responses like that, I unintentionally influenced Erin to think of herself as a black sheep—I influenced her to think that she did not fit in. As a result, I think her weaknesses loomed larger in her eyes than her strengths did, which diminished her sense of self-worth.

As parents, one of our greatest goals should be to appreciate each member of the family for the differences God created in them, and then to find unity in similar pursuits and goals. This means you love and accept the kids you have—and inspire them to grow into the people that God created them to be.

No, your child may not grow up exactly as you imagined, but he or she will grow up to be exactly who God imagined. Exactly who He intended. Exactly who He created.

And that is most important.

Discover Your Kids' Gifts

A woman came into my office in tears. She told me that her son, Caleb—a senior in high school—was drifting away from his goals, and she was worried he was ruining his life.

I asked her to elaborate. She explained that Caleb had told them he wanted to apply to art school instead of business school. She also said that he was talking about taking an unpaid internship at an art gallery that summer instead of working to earn money for college. She explained further that he seemed flighty and day-dreamy and out of touch at home, instead of diligent, hardworking, and goal-oriented, as he had always been before.

"He's always wanted to be a businessman," she said. "He was four years old when he declared he wanted to follow in his father's footsteps. We set out a plan for him, and he has always followed it until recently."

"And what about art?" I asked.

"Oh, that's just a hobby," she quickly said and then looked at her feet.

Caleb's mom—like so many parents I meet—had fallen into the trap of defining what she thought her son needed for his life without considering his personal desires, likes, dislikes, talents, and skills.

I asked her, "Is he good at art?"

"Yes! Of course!" She smiled. "But he can't ever make money doing that. He has to focus on a real-life skill."

You are probably shaking your head at Caleb's mom right now—and rightfully so—but I want to ask you a tough question. Have you ever done the same to your kid? I have. I wanted Erin to be a calm, collected introvert instead of the passionate, creative extrovert God made her.

We have to accept and love the kids we have (relate). We have to work hard to uncover all the wonderful things that our kids have to offer (inspire). We have to foster appreciation for each kid's unique personality and character (inspire). And we have to work hard to resolve the conflicts that our differences bring about (teach and equip).

This means two things. First, it means we have to accept that our kids are who they are and work to embrace that rather than to change it. That means if your kid wants to be an artist, you sign him up for art classes. But it also means that you allow each child's special gifts, talents, desires, character traits, and personality to determine their role in your family dynamics.

Quick Tips for Understanding Your Kid's Unique Purpose

1. You don't have to treat all your kids the same. Equally love, cherish, and connect with them, yes, but not in the same way. For example, in our family Erin has always been the connector. She's emotionally intuitive, so when someone is upset, she always knows, and she finds a way to connect. When she was younger, we looked at her emotional intuition as a bad trait—she was always pushing conflict forward, driving it to a breaking point—but now we see it as a good thing. She's always the one who will call a family meeting to talk things through. She plans family events. She finds ways for us to be together. Her role in our family dynamics was and is the connector.

2. Allow your kids to grow into roles that suit them. If you have a child who is mathematically minded and organized, let him help you set the grocery budget and plan meals as one of his chores. If you have a child who is creative and artistic, let her become your interior decorator. The child who is a musician can set up a family music-appreciation class every night at dinner and share a favorite tune. And the child who is a scientist can be in charge of the garden.

3. Allowing your kids to develop their strengths and assume suitable roles goes beyond chores and household living. It builds family character and insight. The child who tends to withdraw from conflict or conversation can be taught to journal his thoughts and prayers. The one that tends to be flighty can be asked to lead the family in story. The child who tends to argue can lead a family debate.

4. Discover when and how each child is most apt to open up and communicate with you. Erin and Alisa enjoyed talking around the dinner table, while Troy preferred to eat silently. Troy seemed to withdraw

from our dinner conversations, but when we got him by himself, his thoughts and emotions would come tumbling out—almost in a rush. We learned to schedule uninterrupted time with him because he needed to be alone with Glen or me, away from the chatter of his sisters, who would dominate the conversation.

5. Once your kids have made a profession of faith in Jesus, explore their unique giftedness by having them take a spiritual gifts inventory. This is a great way to bring joy to their Christian experience by helping them discern and then exercise the gifts God has given them.

Don't change your kids. Love them into becoming the men and women God designed them to be. Embrace their strengths, help them grow in their weak areas, and connect with them about what they love and in ways that support them individually. Allow God to open your eyes to the big plans He has for your babies. They are His children first, and He knows them intimately, so set your mind to discovering how their Creator designed each of them.

God does not make mistakes. Even our weaknesses have purpose. Our strengths can make us proud, but it's in our weaknesses that we recognize our need for Jesus and humbly learn to rely on Him.

Chapter 12

The Motive Behind the Madness

Ellen

ASHER WAS FAILING.

He was failing eighth-grade English, making only 43 percent, and he was on the edge in science, history, and, according to his parents, life in general.

Lindsay and Clayton, Asher's parents, came to me with tears in their eyes and told me that their bright, articulate child had slipped. Asher had always been a strong student. In elementary school, he had been known as "the perfect little boy." He had filled a tiny green journal with stories and poems, which he kept under his pillow. He had wanted to become a famous writer and had told everyone about his dream. And that was not all. He had rarely missed a math problem on tests. He had been the top reader in his class. And he had earned belt after belt in karate classes, accomplishing more than most kids his age and at a much quicker pace. Asher had seemed to have it all—talent, drive, and a great personality.

But then things changed. In seventh grade, Asher asked to drop out of karate. He told his parents he was tired of it, he didn't want to spend his afternoons at the studio when he could be hanging out with friends, and he didn't really feel the drive for martial arts anymore. His parents let him quit—the last thing they wanted was to push him to do something he wasn't interested in.

After that, his grades started to slip. Math homework—which had once come easily to him—became a nightly battle. Asher felt that his math problems were too hard. Lindsay had spent hours and hours sitting with him as he stared at a blank page, refusing even to start working the problems. She told of a night that her son screamed, "I'm just not good at math!" and ran to his room.

But then came the straw that broke the camel's back. Asher had always been a fantastic writer—as you remember, he dreamed of becoming a novelist. He had been one of those rare kids who got excited when papers were assigned—and who spent hours working and reworking the pages until they seemed perfect. And his eighth-grade English essay was no exception. Asher had worked hard. He had come up with a concept, prepared a rough draft, edited it, and then finalized the paper into something that he liked.

On the day the paper was due, Lindsay had asked him to make sure it was in his folder in his backpack (it was) and dropped him off at school. Later that day, she got a call from the teacher. Asher hadn't turned in the paper, and he was now failing eighth-grade English. When Lindsay picked him up from school that day, she immediately pulled him aside and asked what had happened. She asked if the paper might have slipped behind the teacher's desk or gotten lost in a pile of papers. But Asher only shrugged and said he had thrown it away.

Asher sighed and explained to his mom that when he had arrived at school, he had realized that they were supposed to attach a signed checklist to the front of the paper—one that checked off the steps, like the rough draft, the editing, and the final draft. Since he had forgotten the checklist, he had just tossed his paper in the wastebasket on the way in to school.

Lindsay was baffled, as was his teacher. The checklist wasn't even part of the grade. It was merely a guide for the students. They were confused, but I wasn't. As soon as I heard the story, I knew what was wrong: Asher is a perfectionist—a very driven perfectionist.

I'll get to my reasoning for thinking that in a minute, but before I do, I want to assert here that there are *lots* of perfectionistic kids like Asher. They are labeled lazy or unmotivated and angry or volatile. They are thought impulsive or naughty or brooding or wild. But these kids are rarely those things. They are perfectionists. Or they are kids who struggle with feelings of self-worth or with depression. Or they are kids who simply can't figure out how to exercise self-control. They are kids who do all sorts of crazy things that their parents and teachers can't figure out . . . but there is motive behind their madness. And it's rarely what people assume it is.

Dig Deeper into Your Kids' Lives

When I told Asher's parents that their son was a perfectionist, they laughed at me—like flat-out belly laughed. And I can see why.

In my years as an educator, I've learned that often the kids who struggle to get by in school or who actually fail classes are not lazy or unmotivated but perfectionistic. There are many legitimate reasons kids struggle in school, such as learning disabilities or environmental difficulties, but if a sudden slip or a refusal to even try should arise, that can be a sign that something besides a struggle is going on.

I explained this to Asher's parents, and the light came on in their eyes. They had both seen their son's drive, his talent, and his ability, and they had both seen him shut it off. Together, we came up with a plan to help him. We talked about his behaviors (throwing away his term paper) being responses to the anxiety he was feeling about inadequacy. We addressed the heart of the issue and—lo and behold—he slowly started performing better. Things changed.

I see this mistake again and again as I work with parents: they jump to conclusions and miss the mark. Parents are good at noticing their kids' troubles, but kids are good at masking the real issues. The little behaviors that pop up often disguise the issues, rather than highlight them. Because of this, one of the first things I ask parents to do is figure out whether what they are assuming about their kids is really what is going on.

Be Really Observant

When my grandson Joey was a toddler, he hit a meltdown point around ten every morning. He cried and screamed and disobeyed, and my daughter soon came to her wit's end. She attributed his behavior to "the terrible twos" and not enough sleep, and she tried everything she could think of to help him. She put him down for early naps, took him outside for exercise, and gave him quiet time in his room, but nothing seemed to cure his midmorning crash. Then, one day, I had Joey on an outing around that time, and since I'm the grandma, I took him to Starbucks for a chocolate milk. He slurped it down and then behaved like an angel for the rest of the morning.

When my daughter and I talked, we realized that every day Joey—an early riser—was having breakfast at six, and by ten, he was starving. His behavior was a result of a blood sugar drop. And since, at that point, it was way too early for lunch, my daughter hadn't even considered that he might be hungry. Of course, she was very hard on herself for not catching on (her poor baby!). But the truth is, it's easy to watch our kids' behavior and, in the heat of the moment, assume intent or motive when the issue is something else. Because of this, I think the first step in looking at your child's heart is to observe him or her.

I want to encourage you to watch each of your kids, know them as individuals, and try to understand them. Watch what happens in the moments that lead up to certain behaviors. Take some notes (maybe when no one's watching so you don't look like a 007 spying on them) and see if a pattern pops up. Maybe your kid is hungry. Maybe he or she is tired. Maybe, like Asher, your kid panics when something goes wrong.

Uncover the Real Issue

Remember the story I told you in chapter 3 about Taylor moving in with her boyfriend and dropping out of school? I encouraged her parents to start with step one of RITE, relate. I asked them to intentionally observe her during the process: to think about what made her tick and to watch how she related to others.

And they observed that Taylor was a people-pleaser. They watched at restaurants as Taylor hesitated to ask a waitress to cook her steak for just a little bit longer. And they watched her allow her friends to walk all over her. They even watched her cancel plans she had to go to a study group one night in order to watch her boyfriend's son so he could go to a movie with friends . . . and then cry as soon as he walked out the door.

Taylor was the quintessential nice girl. Everyone said so. She was just nice—nice to teachers, to friends, to siblings—nice to everyone. And this is a good thing! God created Taylor with a tender, merciful, kind heart that yearned to make others happy. But Taylor was experiencing anxiety over how to make others happy and how to deal with their disappointment when she failed to do so. She was having a hard time saying no to people out of fear that they would be disappointed in her. And she was having a hard time standing up for herself when people asked too much of her.

She so badly wanted to please her boyfriend that she said yes to things he wanted even if she had to act against her conscience. Her parents confronted her after they heard she was having sex with him. She then confessed her hurt and anger with herself over disappointing them, and she explained that that was why she had cut off all contact with them.

So while her actions—sexual promiscuity, drinking, and dropping out of school—looked like pure rebellion, they weren't. The truth was, the issue ran much deeper than that. Taylor lacked a sense of personal boundaries. This root cause didn't excuse her sin, but it did give her parents a specific thing to work on. They had to give her some tools for protecting her heart— her merciful, kind heart—and for dealing with her feelings of inadequacy when she felt like she had disappointed someone.

This new insight gave Taylor's parents something positive to focus on in their conversations with her and something they could pray for. It wasn't an end-all solution, but it was a way to connect with Taylor and to help her move past her struggles.

And you can break through with your kids, too. Instead of automatically attributing your kids' sin to rebellion, disobedience, laziness, disrespect, or dishonesty, dig deeper. Consider other factors. Observe their God-given personality traits, their struggles, and the triggers that cause outbursts of anger or withdrawal. And consider how all of this influences their behavior.

Every single one of us has sinned and fallen short of the glory of God. None of us is perfect, none of us is holy, none of us is able to calmly manage the trials and tribulations of life with grace and mercy every day—especially when we haven't had our coffee. This is true, but the fact that we all know Romans 3:23 and quote it often can actually hinder our parenting. Let me explain. As parents, we tend to label problems as sin—which they are—and then stop there. We don't think to dig deeper to find the root cause behind the behavior.

Consider the Alternative Label

Asher's parents assumed that Asher was inherently lazy, when in reality he was struggling with anxiety related to perfectionism. Taylor's parents assumed she was rebellious and not seeking God, when in reality she was choosing to please others instead of God. Both kids were struggling. And both were mislabeled. To connect with their hearts—and to help them overcome—their parents needed to dig a little deeper and find out what character quality was motivating the behavior glaring on the surface.

And there are millions of other struggling kids out there, who have been mislabeled by parents, teachers, coaches, and Sunday school leaders. Here are a few examples:

- A child labeled disobedient or rebellious may have sensory processing issues or ADHD and need support with impulse control.
- A kid labeled discontent or a complainer could be struggling with depression or anxiety.
- A child labeled dishonest or sneaky may be struggling with anxiety or panic attacks.
- A kid labeled careless or messy could need help learning to follow step-by-step instructions.

- A child labeled rude or disruptive may have Asperger's syndrome or social anxiety.

This list could go on and on. I would like to say that reality is simple, but actually it's very complicated. Beautifully complicated. God created each of us—and each of our kids—with a beautiful, complex, layered personality, which is full of emotions, talents, strengths, and weaknesses. Because of this, our kids' behavior is complex. It's nuanced. And it often has multiple causes and multiple solutions.

My grandson Will provides a perfect example of how complex a child's behavior can be. For years, his parents had gotten calls from teachers and coaches and Sunday school leaders saying he was tough to have in class. He tended to be aggressive when he got frustrated, pushing or hitting kids in class. He'd squeeze kids tightly or hug them until he hurt them. He also acted squirrely, often getting out of his seat or not raising his hand to talk.

My daughter had no idea what to do. She talked to him about being kind to other kids and not hurting them. She gave consequences. She made him practice sitting still and showed him examples of how to behave in school. And nothing seemed to work.

And then the answer came from the most unexpected situation: Will got a concussion. My daughter and I walked outside one morning and found him lying facedown in our driveway. My daughter rolled him over and started tickling him, thinking he was fake sleeping. Then he opened his eyes and immediately threw up. We raced him to the hospital. His eyes were crossed and his head was drooping.

At the hospital, they did a CT scan, diagnosed a concussion, and checked him in for observation. A few minutes later, the nurse came in and asked if she could check his hands and arms. She said that if a kid falls hard enough to get a concussion, they typically scrape their hands and elbows or break their wrists. But Will's hands and arms were fine. The doctor was baffled but assumed that Will had gotten knocked unconscious or had fallen at a weird angle. Will healed. We moved on.

Then it happened again. This time at a playground. Will fell backward off a wall and hit his head. Same story: a rush to the hospital, vomiting, a diagnosed concussion, and not a scrape on his elbows or arms.

This time, the doctor referred Will to a neurologist, who did a series of tests and discovered something very interesting: Will's reflexes weren't working normally. When children fall, they will reflexively reach out and catch themselves with their arms. But Will didn't. Instead, his arms reflexively move backward, leaving him vulnerable to head trauma.

Here's where things get interesting. You may be wondering what this has to do with Will misbehaving in school, and I will tell you. After the diagnosis, the neurologist referred Will to an occupational therapist for testing, and it was discovered that the reflex issues were related to sensory processing issues. Occupational therapy started to correct the reflex issues and—lo and behold—Will's behavior improved.

Because his sensory processing issues have been addressed, not only is he safer on the playground, but he is better able to sit still in class, and he is less aggressive and less defiant. That isn't to say his behaviors weren't problems—they were—but the cause behind his behaviors was different from what most people thought.

Address the Root Cause

Once you have watched, dug deeper, uncovered the real issue, and considered the label, the best way to disciple your kids—not discipline, but disciple—is through connected, prayerful, focused conversation that addresses the issue behind the issue. This doesn't mean that there won't be consequences for their actions—Asher, for example, failed eighth-grade English and had to take summer school—but rather that you will equip your kids with tools that will help them perform better in the future.

Apply the RITE Plan

When your kid is misbehaving—especially in a situation where he or she has layered motives and mixed-up reasoning—you have a perfect opportunity to use the RITE plan. RITE helps you connect with their hearts, identify the motive behind their actions, strategize, and supply effective tools for moving forward.

Start by relating to your child. "Yes, Asher, we are really sad you threw away your English paper, too. We saw you working so hard on that. Can you tell us what you were doing?" Then listen—without judging, without lecturing, without rolling your eyes and making him feel like he made the biggest mistake of his life.

Then inspire. "Asher, this is not the end! This doesn't mean you can never be a writer or that you won't graduate from high school. This is just a tiny bump in the road. We can get through this together."

And next you teach. "Asher, we have a feeling you didn't throw away that paper because you just felt like tossing it aside. There must have been much more going on there. We've been looking into perfectionism, and we think you are a perfectionist! This is good! It's the way God made you, and it shows us that He made you to do great things. But it can also cause problems like this one. Would you like to hear about some of the stuff we've been reading and why we think you are a perfectionist?"

And finally, you equip. "Asher, let's work together to come up with some tools that can help you when you are feeling panicky about your work."

With this strategy, kids who could have otherwise been labeled lazy or unsuccessful or defiant or disobedient or rebellious get the tools they need to move forward. They also build a strong connection with their parents and strengthen their desire to follow God. And parents are able to give up yelling, nagging, and grounding their kids and start addressing the issues with connectivity and hope.

Win-win in my book.

Quick Tips for Helping Your Unique Kids

1. Memorize verses. The Bible is God's Word for us, which means that between those pages you can find tools made specifically for you that

will address your family's heart issues. Choose a few verses about character, honesty, perfectionism, or anxiety and memorize them as a family.

2. Give your kids tools. So very often, I find that kids who make bad choices do so because they don't have the necessary tools to help them make good choices. For example, Asher chose to throw away his paper because he panicked when he realized it wasn't perfect. We came up with a strategy for him to use whenever he starts to feel panicky. He takes a deep breath, texts his mom to tell her he needs to be talked down from a ledge, and he doesn't make any decisions until she responds. In return, she doesn't get angry but helps him talk through the situation. That plan is a tool. Discuss with your kids similar tools that can help them when they have to make decisions, such as counting to ten, phoning a friend, or praying.

3. Institute coffee or tea talks. You're never going to work through a tough issue in the heat of the moment. So set aside time each week for a "coffee talk" with your kid. During this time, pray, talk, share stories, share struggles, and come up with strategies to help overcome your kid's struggles. Let this be a calm, uplifting time you share together, not a time of lectures or nagging or consequences. A friend of mine has established "tea time" for heart-to-heart chats with one or another of her kids. They have learned to look forward to these occasions because they know they will have their mom's undivided attention and, over a cup of tea, they will have a chance to safely share their thoughts and feelings.

4. Use media. Buy books and watch movies together, and then talk about what is in them. If your kid is struggling with dishonesty, buy him a novel with a character who is dishonest and learns from it. Watch a movie together about a person who learns that deceit never pays. If your kid is struggling with anxiety, buy her a book about anxiety. Watch a movie about a character who learns to move past fear. Let your kids read good, Christian stories about imperfect people

who struggle, and watch quality movies with thought-provoking themes.

5. Pray. Often when kids struggle, it is evidence that God is working in their hearts. So the most powerful thing you can do as parents is pray. Pray that God will give you insight and wisdom. Pray that their God—the God who created them to be great warriors for His kingdom—would work in their hearts and help them overcome their problems. Pray diligently. And allow God to do His work.

Every single kid needs a unique plan to help him or her grow and thrive. But special kids—the ones who have been gifted with big personalities and (sometimes) big struggles—need even more focus. I've often said that some of the best kids I've ever worked with—the ones who grow up to be warriors of the faith—are the ones who, at an early age, were labeled "difficult" or "special needs." So I encourage you to trust God's plan: He made your child the way He made him or her for a reason, and He loves him or her more than you can imagine.

Jesus has big plans for your kid. And He's not going to let a little bit of misbehavior or some wild-and-crazy behavior change His plans.

Chapter 13

The Use of Story

Glen

I LOVE TO IMAGINE what it would have been like to be one of Jesus's disciples. I imagine conversing on long, dusty walks, watching as crowds gathered around, and receiving awe-inspiring revelations. One of the things I would have enjoyed most were Jesus's stories. I can just picture myself sitting at His knee, munching on a loaf of crusty bread, and listening to Him share God's purposes and desires for my life through stories and hearing Him speak in meaningful parables.

I think the art of storytelling—perfected by Jesus—is one of the most important skills we can have as teachers, parents, and grandparents. I'm going to throw in some teacher talk here—I can't help it after spending forty-two years as an educator. If we want to teach and inspire our kids effectively, we have to honor the way they were designed to learn. And as Jesus demonstrated by telling more than forty-five parables, human beings learn best when they are able to relate to what they are learning. This means, if we want our kids to learn from us, we have to tell a lot of stories.

In Matthew 13:10–13, Jesus explains why stories are so powerful:

The disciples came up and asked, "Why do you tell stories?"
He replied, "You've been given insight into God's kingdom.

You know how it works. Not everybody has this gift, this insight; it hasn't been given to them. Whenever someone has a ready heart for this, the insights and understandings flow freely. But if there is no readiness, any trace of receptivity soon disappears. That's why I tell stories: to create readiness, to nudge the people toward receptive insight." (MSG)

Needless to say, I love telling stories. I believe that my role as a teacher or grandparent or parent goes much deeper than just teaching facts and figures. It's about speaking to a kid's heart. And I use story to do that—to inspire purpose, to set a vision, and to show kids, instead of telling them, how they should act and what they should do.

This chapter is about the power of story in helping kids grow in the ways God desires. It's about helping kids find their unique gifts and strengths and then finding opportunities to exercise them in the world. It's about giving the next generation a reason to engage—with God, with family, and with their future. And it's about giving kids relevant ideas that will inspire them to dream big and become warriors in God's kingdom.

And since humans learn best through story, I'm going to take this opportunity to share with you three of my favorites, which I use to set a godly vision for my kids, grandkids, and students. I hope this chapter will illustrate for you how you can use your own stories to help your kids learn, grow, and thrive. Stories can fulfill all four parts of the RITE plan—they can help you relate to your kids, inspire your kids, teach your kids, and equip your kids.

Before I share the stories, I have to be completely up front with you: These aren't original stories. I heard the first one from my own teacher when I was a high school kid. (It didn't have the computer stuff in it way back then, but the main point was the same.) I have no idea where he got it, but I have a feeling that many versions of this story have been passed down for generations. The other stories were told to me on my parents' or even grandparents' knees. They are generational stories, stories that are part of the moral fiber of our country.

That said, these are my versions. I have taken the stories that I learned from my own parents and grandparents and teachers and friends and made them my own. I've turned them into "Mr. Schuknecht parables," if you will—stories that I feel give my students a vision to hook on to and a focus for their work.

I encourage you to do the same. Make your own versions of these stories. Or come up with your own stories. Use them. Share them. Tell them. And give your kids something to consider as they start to see the vision God has for their future.

Teach Kids to Work Hard

I think every math teacher has heard this about a million times: "I'm not a mathematician! I want to be a rapper when I grow up, so why do I need to understand trigonometry?" I hear it every year. At least twice (a day). And I always have a ready response the first time a student says this. Why? Because I believe our kids should work to be the best they can be at whatever it is they are doing. Sure, a professional singer likely won't use trigonometry on a daily basis, but she will use hard work and problem-solving skills. And the brain is like a muscle (well, kind of)—the more you use it, the stronger it gets. Thinking hard makes your brain stronger, and unfortunately the opposite is also true. I teach my kids that every day is an opportunity to work hard and to get better. And I teach them this lesson (and this vision) through this story.

Sarah graduated from the University of Texas (Hook 'em, Horns!) with a degree in graphic design. She had worked really hard in school—earning top honors and creating a portfolio that she hoped would cause a big advertising agency to want to hire her. She had big dreams and plans for her future—a condo downtown by the river, a job she loved, and a paycheck that would enable her to pay off her college loans in just a few years.

Then the economic crash happened. What bad luck for Sarah. After working so hard for so long, she found that no one was hiring, not even the little firms in the suburbs. After months of searching, Sarah couldn't pay her rent. She took a job waiting tables for the lunch shift at a Tex-Mex place downtown.

One day at lunch, two men and two women in business suits came to one of her tables. She smiled as she served them chips and queso and white chicken enchiladas, all while secretly weeping inside and wishing she were the one in the power suit with the powerful job.

At the end of lunch when Sarah brought their check to the table, one of the executives asked her, "How long have you been working here? You do a really great job."

She smiled and responded, "I've been here for a few months, and I really love it here. The job is fun, and the people are great. I had big dreams of being a graphic designer—I even got my degree at UT in graphic design— but I couldn't get a job. So I'm here."

He nodded. The executives paid their check and left.

Sarah went to clean their table and found a note and a business card on top of her tip. "Sarah, thank you for your great service today. I am the HR manager at the PGR Ad Agency. I would like to interview you for an open graphic design job we have. Could you come in tomorrow morning at nine?"

After I tell this story, I ask my kids if anyone has ever told them that they are just waiting for God to open the right doors. If they say yes, my response is always the same: God doesn't open doors. He is the key keeper. Sometimes He unlocks doors for us, but we are responsible for turning the knobs. Other times He actually locks doors. He keeps the key and directs us toward other doors. And still other times, He opens doors, but only just a crack, as if they are held by a chain like those on hotel doors. He may even open doors wide for us but then slam them back shut. But if we are willing to step forward and jiggle those doorknobs—that is, to work hard to get prepared—then our doors will open gloriously if the key keeper deems it right.

I tell my students that their job is to pray diligently, to dream big, to work hard, and then to work even harder. They must stay positive and do the best they can at whatever it is they are called to do. They must be kind, show empathy, and prepare for those times when the Great Key Keeper unlocks a lock and allows them to swing the door wide open.

Teach Kids to Take the Hard Road

When I talk to my students about diligent work, I explain that, in my class, they are expected to show their work on all problems (even if they already know the answer in their head) and that proper headings and neat hand-writing are required. (Because I said so, that's why!) I tell them I expect neat, organized, complete work. And they moan and groan, and grumble that I am obviously still stuck in the nineteenth century, before they even knew about calculators. They act like I'm the meanest teacher ever, practi-cally asking them to fish with their hands. And that's when they usually ask why they have to do it the hard way. But I stand by my requirements: neat, complete, correct work. Here's the story to prove it.

My four-year-old grandson, Asa, wet the bed for three consecutive nights. Now, for many four-year-olds this would be normal, but it was very abnormal for Asa. He had decided he didn't want to wear diapers ever again and then never had another accident. He easily made it through the night without a pull-up by the age of three.

Needless to say, my daughter was beyond frustrated.

But on night number four, she overheard Asa talking to his sister, Alma. "You know, if you just pee in your bed, then you don't have to wash your hands."

Alma nodded, her eyes lighting up. "I no like washing hands."

My daughter stopped that conversation really fast. Sure, peeing in bed seemed like a shortcut to Asa and Alma, but getting up and changing the sheets was definitely no shortcut for their mom.

Fortunately, Asa quickly learned that a shortcut is usually not really a shortcut when his mom made him get up at two in the morning to help clean the sheets and take a shower. And there haven't been any bedwetting incidents since.

I have a poster hanging in my classroom that says, "A shortcut is often the quickest way to somewhere you weren't going." And this is something I remind my students of over and over, because I think that taking shortcuts is one of our youth's biggest problems today.

In classrooms, kids struggle with academic integrity on a daily basis. Instead of taking the time to learn the material and do quality work, kids find and buy papers on the Internet. They plagiarize the work of others. They write cheat notes on their arms or legs. Likewise, kids on sports teams and in drama troupes and art classes cut corners and skip practices. They are looking for ways to make their lives easier, but in the long run, they are making them harder.

I remind my kids that shortcuts don't pay off in the long run. Shortcuts don't produce the integrity that will be required by their families and their workplaces. And they don't result in the perfection of a craft. Really great athletes, musicians, actors, and artists whom we admire didn't take short-cuts to get where they are. They worked hard to perfect their craft so that, now, they are able to make their work look effortless. And so must everyone else.

We have to teach our kids to train their minds to recognize the tendency to take shortcuts and then to turn themselves in a different direction. I have my students practice purpose-driven self-talk—words that will help them resist shortcuts and do what is right, no matter how hard things get. I teach them that when a certain assignment or practice or project or competition gets tough, they should think of phrases like these:

- Yes, it would be easier to just copy this paper on the Internet, but I'm not the kind of person who chooses what's easy. I'm the kind of person who chooses what's right.
- I can do this! And I will be so much better at math/soccer/English/ painting when I'm done.
- This is the moment when things get hard. And this is the moment where I'm going to choose to rise to the occasion.

- Shortcuts are the fastest way to get where I'm not going. So I'm going to go ahead and just keep taking the long road.

I have seen a lot of success with this strategy. Our kids know what is right. And most of them want to do what is right. So if we give them the tools to stay on the right track, they often do what is right.

And they get to where they are going in a way that fills them with integrity, purpose, and hope.

Teach Kids to Persevere

Every year, I have a student or two who tries to do the last-minute grade dance. They spend the first seven weeks of a nine-week term goofing around in class, doing their best to do as little work as possible. And then a light bulb goes on! Grades are due. Report cards will soon be out. And suddenly the former slacker student becomes the most dedicated kid in the class.

"Mr. Schu! Is there any extra credit I can do over the weekend?"

"Mr. Schu! I stayed up until two o'clock studying last night and still got up at six to study some more!"

And, perhaps my favorite, "Mr. Schu! I baked you some chocolate chip cookies last night just out of the goodness of my heart."

Sadly, the tactic never works. I feel bad for these kids; yes, I do. But usually it's just too late for them to catch up. All of us have heard the saying, "All is well that ends well." In my classes, I say, "All is well that begins and ends well." Because the truth is that on any task, you need both bookends to succeed—a strong start and a strong finish. Here's a story I tell that demonstrates this.

The Texas Tornadoes football team had a losing streak three seasons long. They had literally lost every single game they had played for three years. And it would have been four seasons, but a team from the next town over had been forced to forfeit a game after a nasty flu outbreak, giving the Tornadoes a single win in four years of Texas football.

As the team sat in the locker room licking their wounds from yet another thumping, an old man with a big, black cowboy hat knocked on the locker room door.

"Can I come in, Coach?" the man asked. "I have something I want to say to the team."

"Sure." The coach didn't know the man well, but he knew he was the owner of a car dealership in town, and he figured whatever he said to the boys wouldn't make them any worse off than they already were.

"Hello! I'm Rowdy Hamilton, and I own the Ford dealership in town. I see on the schedule that next week you guys are playing the Bulldogs from across town. They haven't lost a single game this season."

The kids booed.

"I'm a proud Tornado. Back in '68 we won the state championship! I still walk by the school every now and again to see that trophy. I sit in these stands every week and watch you guys play. And I'm tired of watching you lose. So I have a proposition for you. If you guys can beat the Bulldogs next week, I will give every single boy on this team a brand-new Ford truck. And there's one for you, too, Coach."

The room was silent.

Then the boys started to murmur. New trucks for everyone? Suddenly there was something worth playing for. They began to cheer and chant. The coach returned to the front of the room and smiled. "Looks like we have some work to do, boys!"

He shook Mr. Hamilton's hand and told the boys that if they wanted to win, they would have to get started the next day. They scheduled an eight o'clock practice for Saturday morning. Not a single boy in the room complained.

The week was amazing. Every kid showed up for practice every day, on fire and ready to work. They ran hard, they perfected plays, and they stayed after practices for hours to watch game film from the Bulldogs. Even the team managers caught the excitement and stayed late to shine every helmet. The coaches spent hours studying film and coming up with a surefire game plan.

And when Friday night rolled around, not only was the team pumped up and excited but they were stronger, faster, and more cohesive than they had ever been. The electricity in the air that night probably hadn't been felt since the glory days of Mr. Hamilton's team. The stadium was packed. Everyone wanted to see the Tornadoes get their big win and new trucks. And everyone wanted to see the Bulldogs lose, which is why the entire stadium fell silent when the final gun sounded and the scoreboard read 49 to 0. The Bulldogs had not merely won but had crushed the Tornadoes despite all their energy, excitement, and hard work.

When the team returned to the locker room, the coach shook his head and said probably the wisest words they had ever heard: one week of hard work will never do the trick. You have to start well, stay well, and end well. The boys were sad. But they learned an important lesson: hard work isn't a one-time event.

The next July, when Coach posted two-a-day practices for the team, a record number of kids showed up. The kids worked harder. They ran faster. They listened better. And you know what? The Tornadoes won two games that next season. And in the season after that, they had a winning record—all because of some Ford trucks that they didn't win.

After this story a football player usually raises his hand and asks me (a) if Mr. Hamilton really would have given all the boys a truck, and (b) if Mr. Hamilton happens to be a real person living in our town. Everyone laughs and giggles and wishes that someone would walk into our team's locker room with the same offer.

I always tell them that this is an urban legend but that the point remains true: if you start talking numbers, it all adds up (I can't help it; I'm a math guy). Research from the Violin Academy in Europe shows that in order to be a master in any area, you need about ten thousand hours of hard, diligent practice. Numerous other researchers have replicated this study, and the number stays about the same for things like sports and careers that need mastery. To put that number in perspective, if you practiced two hours a day, seven days a week, for fourteen years, you would reach ten thousand hours. It's not something that happens in a week or a year or even a decade.

Being a champion takes hours and hours of hard work—no shortcuts, no take-a-few-months-off, no procrastinating—just dedication, drive, and effort. And a little help from guys like Rowdy Hamilton.

Quick Tips for Storytelling (Even If You Aren't a Storyteller)

1. Read Jesus's parables together as a family (maybe during morning devotional time or as bedtime stories) and discuss what each person learned from it.
2. Read bedtime stories every night. Choose great books with good morals that serve as more than entertainment (which sadly means *Captain Underpants* doesn't count).
3. Share your own personal struggles as stories—the time you failed a test or the time you got caught lying—and then discuss with your kids how they could respond differently in a similar situation.
4. Implement family reading time. Choose great books—I recommend starting with The Chronicles of Narnia or similar classics—and read them together as a family. Pause often to discuss the characters and the lessons they are learning.
5. Read great books yourself. Allow stories to seep into your life and share the lessons you learn with your kids.
6. Listen to audiobooks together in the car.
7. Turn your lectures into stories. Next time you are tempted to lecture, try telling a story. Instead of saying, "You need to learn to pick up your toys and keep your room clean," tell your child a story about a little boy who never cleaned his room and whose favorite toy truck got lost under his bed. Keep it simple. But let the story do the talking.
8. Start a family book club—ask everyone in the family to read a certain book and then have book club night with popcorn, treats, and a family book discussion.

9. Dig deeper into stories. Books, TV shows, and even movies are full
    of stories, so whenever your family hears a story, take the time to talk
    about the lessons involved and what could be applied to everyday
    life.

10. Look to the role models. Read stories about people who have gone
    before—men and women who changed the world as writers, ath-
    letes, artists, and heroes of the faith—and consider what they did to
    reach that level of success.

11. Practice purpose-driven self-talk with your kids and grandkids. Show
    your kids how to work out solutions to their problems in their own
    minds.

I know that by weaving story into your family's lifestyle, you can share
God's truth and inspiring examples with your kids. Through storytelling,
you emulate Jesus and bring hope, build resilience, help your kids to think,
and give your kids insight into who God is and who He wants your child
to be.

Chapter 14

The Long-Suffering Love of God

Ellen

AMELIA SAT ACROSS FROM me at the small round table in the back of our neighborhood coffee shop.

Her chai latte was untouched, probably cold now, as she stared down at her hands folded in her lap.

"Aren't you going to drink your latte, Amelia?" I asked, trying to get the conversation started.

Amelia had been an ideal student. Her teachers loved her. Her peers respected her. Her parents were so very proud. She was regarded as someone who would not only succeed in reaching her life goals but also stay true to her beliefs. Hers was a success story, so I was shocked and dismayed to hear that, as a sophomore in college, she had stayed away from church and family, had moved in with her boyfriend, and was frequenting campus parties.

I decided to reach out to Amelia and attempt to rekindle what was at one time a mentoring relationship between us. Surprisingly, she agreed to meet with me.

After a few more minutes of silence, I decided to just dig in, to say what needed to be said.

"What's changed?" I asked her, hoping to break through the ice between us. Her eyes glistened as she opened and closed her mouth several times, as if unsure what to say or how to say it. Finally, the words started to flow.

"I want to fit in," she confided. "Everyone is going to parties. Having sex," she added, "is just part of the normal college experience. And to be honest, I enjoy the freedom. I don't have to try so hard to be approved of. I can relax."

I sat there silently, contemplating Amelia's honest words. I understood her reality. While I had never fallen into the party scene, I had spent my college years striving to win God's approval, and my Christian walk had become anxiety-producing and stifling. I too had longed for something that felt free.

I had learned quickly, however, that the world and its ways brought no freedom. As my own story flashed through my mind, I felt deep compassion and pain for Amelia.

Wanting to have an honest conversation, I asked her, "Do you still believe the Bible to be God's truth?"

She sat silently for several moments before she spoke. "Of course I do. I just can't seem to let go."

Can't seem to let go. Think about those words. Let them roll around in your head for a bit. This girl—almost a woman—had walked away from the God she knew, and yet our God in His infinite and unbreakable love for His children hadn't reciprocated. He hadn't walked away from her. In fact, He was right there tugging on her precious heart, not letting her let go.

He's a never-give-up, never-let-go, never-stop kind of God. A God who clings tightly to our kids, even if they aren't clinging to him. A God who gives second and third and seventy-seventh chances.

I reached over to Amelia, took her hand, and said, "Amelia, you can't let go because God isn't letting go of you. You are His beautiful, much-loved child, and He has big plans for you. He isn't finished. "

She sniffled and a lone tear streaked down her check.

"But . . . isn't it too late? I mean, God has to be so angry with me. And what about my parents? They will never forgive me." Her words drifted off.

"Amelia, God isn't done with you. He has big plans for your life. And that means not only will He forgive you, He'll continue to pursue you. So what you need to do is press into that can't-let-go feeling. Press into God. Run toward Him, not away from Him. Run toward the ones you have been running away from. And trust that God will do great work with the forgiveness that He has so readily promised each of us."

I wish I could say that Amelia stopped right then and rejected her errant lifestyle, but in truth Amelia just sighed, smiled, and said, "Thanks for meeting with me, Mrs. Schuknecht." And then she left.

In the months that followed, Amelia struggled. There was push and pull. Her convictions went back and forth, and she had good days and bad days. But through it all, God never let go of Amelia. That was evident because she came to talk to me and to her parents again and again. It was evident because she slowly started to break some of her chains, her habits. And it was evident because she once again stepped into the church sanctuary with her family, after months of absence.

That God never let go of Amelia was evident because she gave her life back to Him in repentance and her faith caught fire. Instead of the lukewarm faith she had possessed as a child, it became blazing hot. He never gave up. He never let go, and He never stopped pursuing her.

I believe that Jesus was talking about kids like Amelia when He said, "Come to me, all who labor and are heavy laden, and I will give you rest. Take my yoke upon you, and learn from me, for I am gentle and lowly in heart, and you will find rest for your souls. For my yoke is easy, and my burden is light" (Matt. 11:28–30).

He knew that the struggle, the burden of sin, was heavy. And He knew He was the only one who could take that yoke from us.

The prophet Jeremiah describes this well when he likens a man whose heart has turned away from the Lord to a shrub in the desert. Then he likens the man whose trust is in the Lord to "a tree planted by water": its leaves remain green even when the heat comes, and it does not cease to bear fruit (Jer. 17:5–8).

God doesn't give up on our kids—not when they are two and throwing tantrums in the aisle at Target, not when they are sixteen and throwing tantrums in your kitchen, and not when they are seventy-six and throwing tantrums at the Elks lodge, playing bingo.

Whether our kids are wholeheartedly following Him or rejecting Him, He loves them and will continue to pursue them. Of course, that fact doesn't mean that your kids haven't grown cold-hearted toward Him. Some people may never turn back to God. We are fallen creatures. But God, ever-loving, ever-knowing, ever-seeking, is still there in the hard times. What comfort it brings to my heart—and hopefully to yours—to know that no matter what our kids do, God will not give up on them. He loves your children as His own precious sons and daughters.

And He isn't done fulfilling His purpose in your life or in the lives of your kids.

Move Your Child's Purpose from Doing to Being

A few years ago, my daughter Erin called me in tears. Her son Will was being, let's call it, "strong-willed" and had been a complete terror in their house. He had hit his sister, knocked over a vase full of flowers and shattered glass onto the floor, pulled the cat's tail, and smeared Play-Doh on the leather couch. To top it all off, he didn't even seem contrite or repentant when he got caught and met with the consequences.

"Mom, something is wrong with him!" Erin cried. "He is not like my other kids. He doesn't even seem to care about right and wrong. I think he is going to end up in juvenile detention! My child is going to end up in jail!"

I told her to stop, to take a deep breath, to pause. Will was four years old at the time—hardly a candidate for juvenile detention, even if he did ruin a lovely leather couch. And even if he had done something bad enough to warrant juvy (some kids do!), I would have said the same thing: God has a plan and a purpose for Will's life. And God isn't done.

I think that in the crazy messes of childhood, when our kids are anything but godly, we tend to give up on them. We assume that they don't care, that they are unmoved, that they will always be strong-willed, unrepentant, mean, dishonest, or whatever bad characteristic is showing up in their behavior at that moment.

And the prevailing Christian parenting culture encourages our unfounded assumptions by placing a strong emphasis on teaching parents what they should do to get their children to do what they want them to do. Just think of how many Christian books you've read that tell you to follow a three-step process to assure obedience. It's easy to believe that our kids' behaviors depend on how we parent them.

What's more, this prevailing doctrine is founded in self-improvement and works and cannot sustain anyone spiritually, because it has no power to change a heart. This doctrine is sinking sand. Kids end up feeling unworthy and incapable. Parents end up exhausted and worn down. And we all end up believing that God is a big policeman in the sky enforcing a crime-and-punishment religion, as our hearts struggle against complacency. The spiritual heritage that we desperately seek breaks down under such influence.

But what if we were to take the same vision that God has for our kids? What if we never give up our belief that God made our kids and has a purpose for them? What if, even in those moments of chaos—in the tantrum, the lie, the back-talking, the bad choices—we focus not on what they did but on who they are in Christ?

When Will hit his sister and ruined the couch, I coached my daughter to spend more time focusing on who he is than on what he did. That's not to say that there weren't consequences for his behavior. He had to help clean up the couch, apologize to his poor sister, apologize to the cat, and pick new wildflowers for another vase. But the most important part of this discipline was focusing on this child's identity in Christ.

I coached my daughter to say things like, "Will, I know God created you to be full of energy and life. He gave you so many gifts, including the gift of creativity and the gift of problem solving. So let's talk about how we can turn those gifts into good deeds, deeds that will show God a glimpse of your heart."

I want to remind you that Will was four. He didn't entirely grasp the significance of that conversation. But seeds were planted, and I pray that when Will is eight or twelve or sixteen or twenty, he will understand that he has a purpose from God, which he was perfectly created to fulfill. This conversation will have long-reaching effects. When our kids find their identity in Christ, they will not opt out of their faith, because they will quit striving for a standard that is impossible to achieve in their own strength.

Our hope is grounded in the truth that "[God] does not faint or grow weary; his understanding is unsearchable" (Isa. 40:28). God is never, ever done with us—even when we turn our back to Him, even when we stubbornly choose our own way, even when we rebel against Him. And when we finally turn back, God's forgiveness is available to us. "Though your sins are like scarlet, they shall be as white as snow; though they are red like crimson, they shall become like wool" (Isa. 1:18). In Him there's hope for struggling kids, like Amelia or Will or every single one of your kids.

As parents, we have such great hopes for our children, but as they grow up they can break our hearts in ways we could never have imagined. We must gently guide them so they become who God calls them to be. And we must love them—as they are—because love is the anchor that will eventually steady them. It is also the beacon of hope on the shore of the sea they may be drowning in.

I am privileged to be able to weep with parents in their sorrows, and I also get to rejoice with them when things turn around. More often than not, they do. I have watched God take what may appear to be a complete disaster and miraculously transform it into success. God is the One who performs the miracle of change in our kids' hearts. That's why I confidently look for ways to convey hope, regardless of how dismal a situation may appear. Nothing is impossible with God. "He who began a good work in you will bring it to completion at the day of Jesus Christ" (Phil. 1:6).

The spiritual heritage you wish to pass on is not negated by the mistakes your children make. It may even be stronger as a result of the lessons learned through mistakes and failures. How you manage the down times may very well become your kids' most important memories. So hang in there. Continue to be Christ's ambassador for your children. This is our spiritual heritage: "He has caused us to be born again to a living hope through the resurrection of Jesus Christ from the dead, to an inheritance that is imperishable, undefiled, and unfading" (1 Peter 1:3–4).

I want to end this book with a glimmer of hope for those of you who are weary, for those of you who have spent the day doing battle with a toddler who just won't take a nap or a teenager who just won't get up in the morning, for those of you who have dealt with a back-talking preteen or a lying fourteen-year-old, for those of you who have watched your preschooler run right across the line you drew in the sand, or who have watched your adult son run away from God time and time again. Yes, I want to offer you four words that should serve as the biggest inspiration, the most important piece of parenting advice: God is not done.

God is not done—with you or your kids. He has a plan and a purpose, one that He created for a time just like this. He has a plan for your kids, for your family, and for your spiritual heritage. He has a plan for His kingdom.

Conclusion: The Cinnamon Rolls and a Spiritual Heritage

Ellen

I KEEP CINNAMON ROLLS in the freezer.

Actually, the grandkids say kor-ca-bis-tees in a terrible mispronunciation of the Finnish word for cinnamon rolls, *korvapuusti*. But I know that when a child walks in and asks for a "korcabistee," I should drop whatever it is I'm doing, pull a roll out of the freezer, and pop it in the microwave. Then I usually prepare a pot of cinnamon tea or a cup of cocoa, depending on the child. Sometimes I serve the little meal on my grandmother's pink rose china. But whatever I do, I stop what I was doing and give the child my full, undivided attention.

Yesterday, the child was Joey, my ten-year-old grandson who had "run away from home" because his parents were being "so unreasonable." He walked through my door with a frown clouding his face and flung his shoes onto the porch. He threw himself onto the couch, mumbling, tears shimmering in the corners of his eyes.

"Oma, can I have a korcabistee?"

It was then that I knew he was struggling—that his emotions were flooding his heart in a way that he couldn't control, that he needed time, conversation, prayer, and me. I pulled him to the table, set his plate before him, and pulled up a chair for me.

"What's going on, Joey?"

"My parents just don't get it." His feelings spilled out as he described what had happened. His dad had asked him to do a chore. Joey hadn't wanted to. His dad had asked again. Joey had talked back. Joey had lost a privilege that was really important to him. It was typical preteen misbehavior that I'm sure every parent of a ten-year-old has witnessed.

But I wanted to give Joey a less-than-typical response. It started with prayer. *Dear Jesus, help me to speak to his heart with words from Your heart.*

And then the words came out of my lips. I told Joey a story about Joey's mom when she had been about his age and had back-talked to me and left the house in tears. It was a story of lost privileges, hurt feelings, and, later, a restored relationship.

Then I moved on to confidence. I told my grandson that I believed in him, that I knew his back-talking and arguing weren't characteristic of the person God created him to be. I told Joey that I knew God was working in his heart to refine him through fire, to use these situations to turn him into the man that He had created him to be—a man after God's own heart, a man who loved well, who responded tenderly, who sought God's face in every decision, a man who would one day pass on a spiritual heritage to children and grandchildren of his own.

There were tears over that cinnamon roll. Tears, and a few giggles—and lots of hugs. And a half hour later, when only crumbs remained on that plate, there was a trip back home, an apology, reconciliation—and hope.

A cinnamon roll—korcabistee, whatever you want to call it—has become a symbol of connection, of hope, of spiritual heritage in our family. And I pray that you will be able to find that thing for your family as well. Maybe it will be a certain chair in a certain room where you go to talk, a cup of a certain type of tea, a certain path around the block, or a fuzzy blue blanket with worn edges that can be wrapped around two people at once. Whatever it is, it must create an opportunity for building a spiritual heritage in your family, for connection and conversation and stories and time, for walking down the path of life in a way that intentionally seeks God and seeks resolution.

We fervently hope that the message in the pages of this book has given you hope. We want you to see a bright future for your family and a vision for who your kids are becoming, and most importantly we want you to have a God-given hope that comes with knowing that He is right there with you as you manage the ups and downs of raising a family.

We too have had good days and bad days. We too have weathered storms where nothing seemed to go right and we wondered if our kids had decided to start taking crazy pills. And we too have hope. Because with the Lord, anything is possible. And we pray that together, we can build connected, strong families that serve Him and inspire a new generation of faith warriors.

In our garage, over his workbench, Glen keeps a sign with a poem by an unknown author. We want to leave you with its encouragement.

Take Time

Take time to think;
    it is the source of power.
Take time to read;
    it is the foundation of wisdom.
Take time to play;
    it is the secret of staying young.
Take time to be quiet;
    it is the opportunity to see God.
Take time to be aware;
    it is the opportunity to help others.
Take time to love and be loved;
    it is God's greatest gift.
Take time to laugh;
    it is the music of the soul.
Take time to be friendly;
    it is the road to happiness.
Take time to dream;
    it is what the future is made of.

Take time to pray;
        it is the greatest power on earth.

Starting today, take your first steps toward a spiritual heritage. Intentionally establish relationships with your family and inspire, teach, and equip them. In time, your family will find itself renewed by God's love and by each other's support. Pull away from those things that create division—from rules that don't seem to work, from arguments, from "things we have always done" that just cause pain. Set this book down today with a new-found resolve to build heritage into every word you say, into every decision you make.

A spiritual heritage starts with a cinnamon roll—or a chair, a cup of tea, a long walk, a fuzzy blanket, a hug, a started conversation. And it ends with a connected, loving family that loves God and loves each other.

Ellen's Famous Cinnamon Rolls

For filling: Place ¾ cup real butter in bowl to soften.

Dough: In a large bowl (or mixer with dough hook), combine 2 cups all-purpose flour (I prefer unbleached) and 1 package dry yeast.

Heat 1 cup milk (or buttermilk), ¼ cup sugar, ¼ cup butter, and 1 teaspoon salt until butter melts. Cool to 115–120°F. Add to dry mixture.

Add 2 eggs and beat at low speed for ½ minute, scraping bowl, or mix in by hand. Slowly stir in 1½–2 cups flour and knead with dough hook or by hand. You will know you have added enough flour when the dough does not stick to the bowl or when it is easily kneaded by hand.

Knead on lightly floured surface until smooth: about 8–10 minutes or by dough hook for 6–8 minutes. Shape into a ball and place in greased bowl. Cover with a towel and place in warm, draft-free location. I prefer to place the dough in an ever-so-slightly heated oven (but make sure to turn the oven off!). Let rise until doubled in bulk—about 50–60 minutes.

Punch down and divide in half. Roll each half into a rectangle about 12 x 8 inches in size.

Filling: Mix ¾ cup softened butter, ¾ cup brown sugar, and 1 tablespoon cinnamon. Spread ½ of the mixture onto each rectangle.

Roll up each piece, starting with the long side, and seal seams. Slice each roll into 8–12 rolls, based on the desired thickness. Place rolls, cut side down, in two greased 9 x 11½-inch round baking pans or place all the rolls into a 9 x 13-inch rectangular baking pan. Cover and let rise until doubled in bulk, about 40 minutes.

Bake at 375°F for 18–20 minutes.

Drizzle icing over warm rolls.

Icing Ideas:

- Mix a few tablespoons milk or cream, ½ teaspoon vanilla, and enough powdered sugar to reach desired consistency.
- Mix softened 8-ounce package cream cheese with 3 tablespoons melted butter, 1 teaspoon vanilla, and 1 cup powdered sugar (more, if needed) for a creamier, thicker, and less sweet icing.

Eat warm or divide into individual portions and freeze for later.